# Four Hasidic Masters
## and Their Struggle against Melancholy

UNIVERSITY OF NOTRE DAME
WARD-PHILLIPS LECTURES IN
ENGLISH LANGUAGE AND LITERATURE

Volume 9

Books by

ELIE WIESEL

*Night*
*Dawn*
*The Accident*
*The Town beyond the Wall*
*The Gates of the Forest*
*The Jews of Silence*
*Legends of Our Time*
*A Beggar in Jerusalem*
*One Generation After*
*Souls on Fire*
*The Oath*
*Ani Maamin, a Cantata*
*Zalmen, or the Madness of God*
*Messengers of God*
*Un Juif, Aujourd'hui*
*Four Hasidic Masters*

# *Four Hasidic Masters*
## and Their Struggle against Melancholy

# Elie Wiesel

Foreword
Theodore M. Hesburgh, C.S.C.

University of Notre Dame Press
Notre Dame · London

*Library of Congress Cataloging in Publication Data*

Wiesel, Elie, 1928–
    Four Hasidic masters and their struggle against
melancholy.

    (Ward-Phillips lectures in English language and
literature; no. 9)

    1. Hasidim—Biography.    2. Phinehas ben
Abraham, of Korets, 1726 or 8–1791.    3. Baruch,
of Tul'chin, 1757 (ca.)–1811.    4. Horowitz,
Jacob Isaac, d. 1815.    5. Horowitz, Naphtali Zebi,
1760–1827.    I. Title.    II. Series.
BM198.W5125        296.8'33        78-1419
ISBN 0-268-00944-9

Manufactured in the United States of America

*For*
*my sister Bea*
*who exemplified the best ideals of*
*Hasidic generosity and understanding*

# Contents

Foreword     xi

Rebbe Pinhas of Koretz     1

Rebbe Barukh of Medzebozh     29

The Holy Seer of Lublin     61

Rebbe Naphtali of Ropshitz     97

Background Notes     125

Synchronology     131

# Foreword

It becomes my difficult and yet pleasing task, in this foreword, to convey some sense of the enormous honor which we at Notre Dame felt in experiencing the ninth annual Ward-Phillips Lectures delivered by Elie Wiesel. It is yet a further honor to be able to introduce them to the larger public which this book will reach. In doing these things, however, I am pleased to acknowledge the large measure of guidance which has been furnished by Professor John J. McDonald, who bore responsibility for arranging the event and for bringing it to fruition. And the event was fruitful in ways no one could fully have anticipated. By telling tales about times, places, and people whom we were impoverished for not having known, Elie Wiesel defined and gave us a unique joy. It is a sense of that complex joy which I have now to capture.

One widely known, brief Hasidic tale ends with a catechetical savor as told by Elie Wiesel: "God made man because he loves stories."[1] But who loves

[1] *The Gates of the Forest* (New York: Avon Books, 1967), p. [10].

stories? Man? If so, why is that a sufficient reason for God to make him? Or is it God who loves stories? If so, did He create man in order to have someone to tell Him stories, or is man himself God's story? On these crucial matters the Hasidic tale and Elie Wiesel remain silent. Their silence, however, generates a kind of ambiguity which is appropriate as the subject comes near the core of human aspiration, human fear, and human faith. In this area, as even the most systematic of great theologians know, language strains mightily at its limitations; only ambiguity, paradox, mystery, and stories can do justice to felt truth.

As Elie Wiesel testifies in this book, and as he intensely demonstrated to the Notre Dame community during the three days on which he delivered the lectures which constitute *Four Hasidic Masters*, he is afraid neither of ambiguity, nor of paradox, nor of mystery. Time and again, the Hasidic masters of whom Wiesel speaks end their dialogues with questions rather than with answers, or with answers that are really more questions, though cast in a declarative form. Rebbe Naphtali of Ropshitz tells a story to the Rizhiner in order to demonstrate wisdom, but he tells "a terrible story" that fits no apparent aspect of the context. Both Rebbes respond with laughter, but "what were they laughing at? At whose expense?"[2] The inappropri-

[2] See below, p. 112.

ate story is somehow appropriate, but how? Is wisdom a quality that can live only in the presence of laughter for the Rebbe Naphtali? Yet it is this same jovial Rebbe whom Wiesel calls a melancholy man, a man in whom there was silence as well as laughter. He dies after months of refusing all conversation:

> "Why don't you want to speak, Father," [begs Reb Eliezer].
>
> The old Master stares at him for a long, long moment, and then replies in a slow burning whisper: "I . . . am . . . afraid. Do you . . . understand? Do you understand, Eliezer? I. Am. Afraid."

And then the questions from Wiesel:

> Afraid of what? Of whom? We shall never know.

But then the affirmation from Wiesel:

> But he did.[3]

In this simultaneous affirmation and question, faith and fear, Wiesel spoke to the Notre Dame community in a way that few have or could. Here again is that approach to the vital center that embraces contraries, where decorum consists in the ability to perceive union without losing necessary distinctions. At no point in the dialogue between Wiesel and Notre Dame were the distinctions blurred. The circumstances, after all, were wonderfully rich in paradox. Wiesel spoke as a Hasid, both in the term's more genetic sense of fervent Jew and in its more localized sense of a specific Jewish reli-

[3] See below, p. 120.

gious and cultural tradition. He spoke, that is to say, from a standpoint so totally unfamiliar to the bulk of his audience as to constitute an apparently separate universe of discourse. The names, the places, even his clearly accented cosmopolitan English spoke of Central and Eastern Europe to listeners predominantly, though not exclusively, Western European, and only Western European at several generations' remove. Even more distinctively, Wiesel's references within that Eastern European context were not to the ruling classes, not to classes which show in histories, but to people whom historians have forgotten. These were people whose legendary "palaces" were, "historically," rather larger-than-usual cottages. Their political movements were rarely sufficient to excite even the enormously sensitive jealousy of aristocracies nervous over their foreseen doom at the hands of impending revolutions.

Those words which did not specifically evoke Eastern Europe were often Hebrew, so the sense of distinction was still clear, nor did its clarity diminish through three days. Quite rightly, Wiesel himself insisted upon the distinction. In the midst of the first lecture he broke from his text and said: "I marvel. What *is* a Hasidic Jew doing here? Why am I speaking at Notre Dame, following an introduction by Father Hesburgh? But it is right." And it clearly *was* right, not only for large humane reasons, but simply on the basis of what was, at that moment, occurring in the lecture hall. Fifteen minutes into the first talk, Wiesel had already begun to mold a community of discourse not unlike what one feels must have characterized the *shtible* of a Hasidic master. Here were people listening less out of respect than out of fascination, and out of fascination less with the exotic than with some felt common element that linked speaker and audience beneath never-dissolved differences.

A word easily attached to that common element might be "humanity," but the word would be too easy, because what happened in this dialogue with Wiesel was more specific and stronger than a species sense. Instead we all experienced an honestly constructed union of traditions. Yet, as you will find upon reading the book based on these lectures, there is nothing of systematic theology in that union. Rather, it is constructed from stories woven together into a cable so tautly made that it responds like a musical instrument to the complex nuances of the potential union. Further, the nuances which seem to sound most insistently on the cable group themselves around a motif of waiting. In these lectures it makes little difference that the Jew waits for the Messiah while the Christian waits for the Messiah's Second Coming. Both wait. It is the human condition. It demands a difficult and balanced response. Jew and Christian can learn much from each other about the proper way to wait.

This is not to suggest that Catholic and Hasid gloss the differences which separate them. The

Catholic will yet strive, for example, as a proper goal of his spirituality, to see approaching death in an attitude of hunger for peace in the Lord Jesus Christ. He will see in Rebbe Naphtali's fear a failure of vision . . . if the Rebbe Naphtali were he. And yet, he will also see a deeply and undeniably human feeling in the Rebbe's cogent fear of death, an expressed fear that must necessarily be somewhere in his own experience. The response of Hasid and Catholic to death, or to any other face of the essential, is the same, though the particular side of the response which reaches expression varies as the tradition varies. There is a wholeness in the union of the two traditions, a wholeness which cannot so clearly be gained as long as the traditions remain separate and unable to speak genuinely to one another.

So long as the traditions *do* remain thus apart, the world continues to risk repetition of World War II's Holocaust. The searing horror of that event, it would seem on the face of it, should serve to insure that it be not repeated, but horror guarantees nothing for long. Not even Elie Wiesel's *Night*, and the books of which it is an epitome, can do that. We would like to believe that the fresher the wound the less likely is the chance of a new assault. But it is not true. In fact, it is something like this that Wiesel may be telling us when he renounces the Holocaust as overt subject for any of his books after *Night*. His renunciation is clearly not a retreat. It is, instead, a recognition that the only hope we have for stopping a second Holocaust lies in the building of a genuine spiritual union among peoples, a union strong enough to withstand that dark attraction to chaos which has so often kept humanity in the shadow of its own violence.

Can a second Holocaust be averted? In Jewish tradition, the coming of the Messiah is presaged by the Gog of Magog, whom the Messiah defeats in order to begin his reign. In Christian tradition, the Second Coming is preceded by Armageddon, at which the forces of evil at last will be defeated, leaving the victors to be ushered into paradise. The near coincidence of messianic and apocalyptic traditions shows clearly, both in terms of overt similarity and in terms of more detailed textual criticism. In both traditions, the necessary means to the end is a coming together of all believers. Hasidic tales, however, suggest that only a few just men need come together to bring the Messiah. Three Hasidim who tried were the Seer of Lublin, the Maggid of Kozhenitz, and Reb Mendel of Riminov. Unfortunately, they "could not agree on tactics,"[4] so Napoleon did not become the Gog of Magog and the Messiah did not come to defeat him. Perhaps our generation, like all before it, will not be able to agree on tactics, but we cannot give up the attempt. We must wait and try.

[4] See below, p. 69.

Although the Seer of Lublin failed to bring the Messiah in collaboration with the Maggid of Kozhenitz and Reb Mendel, he had not invested all his energy in that specific attempt, and he did *not* fail to bring the fervor of Hasidism to Lublin. As Rebbe there, he intensified the Jewish life of the community, and the sort of intensity which he brought held promise for future attempts at the Messiah, attempts which will succeed in the generation that will finally be ready to be gathered in. It is that sort of intensity which Elie Wiesel made felt in the Notre Dame community.

This must not be confused with conversion, however. Wiesel made no attempt at, and generated no feeling of, "conversion" in the usual and limited sense of movement from one religious tradition to another. Nor was there "conversion" in an evangelical or revivalist sense. For all the intensity of the experience, there was little overt display of emotion. When Elie Wiesel lectured, he sat at a small table on an otherwise bare stage, speaking quietly and with only the most restrained gestures into a microphone. At moments of most intense communication, he spoke more quietly than ever, it seemed. Yet the intensity was unmistakable, and it came clearly from the union of two separate traditions. These lectures, sounding as if they belonged to a *shtible,* instead came to life in a University that has for decades been engaged in trying to produce a genuine, deeply Christian community of learning.

So there was, after all, a kind of conversion. In whatever way that "conversion" may suggest "converge," there was a conversion to which this book serves as monument and prolongation. We pray that this conversion might be one of the necessary steps toward that larger set of convergences which, accomplished, can confirm us all in an unwavering hope for the Coming.

THEODORE M. HESBURGH, C.S.C.

# Rebbe Pinhas
# of Koretz

Hasidic legend has it that a disciple came to see Rebbe Pinhas of Koretz, known for his wisdom and compassion.

"Help me, Master," he said. "I need your advice, I need your support. My distress is unbearable, make it disappear. The world around me, the world inside me, is filled with turmoil and sadness. Men are not human, life is not sacred. Words are empty—empty of truth, empty of faith. So strong are my doubts that I no longer know who I am—nor do I care to know. What am I to do, Rebbe? Tell me, what am I to do?"

"Go and study," said Rebbe Pinhas of Koretz. "It's the only remedy I know. Torah contains all the answers. Torah *is* the answer."

"Woe unto me," said the disciple, "I am unable even to study. So shaky are my foundations, so all-pervasive my uncertainties, that my mind finds no anchor, no safety. It wanders and wanders, and leaves me behind. I open the Talmud and contemplate it endlessly, aimlessly. For weeks and weeks I remain riveted to the same page, to the same problem. I cannot go further, not even by a step, not even by a line. What must I do, Rebbe, what can I do to go on?"

When a Jew can provide no answer, he at least has a tale to tell. And so Rebbe Pinhas of Koretz invited the visitor to come closer, and then said with a smile: "Know, my young friend, that what is happening to you also happened to me. When I was your age I stumbled over the same obstacles. I, too, was filled with questions and doubts. About man and his fate, creation and its meaning. I was struggling with so many dark forces that I could not advance; I was wallowing in doubt, locked in despair. I tried study, prayer, meditation. In vain. Penitence, silence, solitude. In vain. My doubts remained doubts, my questions remained threats. Impossible to proceed, to project myself into the future. I simply could not go on. Then one day I learned that Rebbe Israel Baal Shem Tov would be coming to our town. Curiosity led me to the *shtibel*, where he was receiving his followers. When I entered he was finishing the *Amida* prayer. He turned around and saw me, and I was convinced that he was seeing me, me and no one else—but so was everyone else in the room. The intensity of his gaze overwhelmed me, and I felt less alone. And strangely, I was able to go home, open the Talmud, and plunge into my studies once more. You see," said Rebbe Pinhas of Koretz, "the questions remained questions. But I was able to go on . . ."

The moral of the story: In the first place, young people ought not to fear questions—provided they have studied before and . . . go on studying after. Secondly, doubts are not necessarily destructive—provided they bring one to a Rebbe.

What did Pinhas of Koretz try to teach his young visitor? One: not to give up; even if some questions are without answers, go on asking them. Two: one must not think that one is alone and that one's inner tragedy is exclusively one's own; others have gone through the same sorrow and endured the same anguish. Three: one must know where to look, and to whom. Four: God is everywhere, even in pain, even in the search for faith. Five: a good story in Hasidism is not about miracles, but about friendship and hope—the greatest miracles of all.

A variation of the same story: Fearing that his faith would be weakened by doubts, Rebbe Pinhas decided to go to Medzebozh to see Rebbe Israel Baal Shem Tov, but the latter just then happened to be visiting Koretz. Rebbe Pinhas ran to the inn where the Baal Shem was staying and heard him explaining to his followers the passage in Scripture describing how Moses stood with his arms raised in prayer, thus strengthening his people to do battle against the Amalekites.

"It happens," said the Master, "that a person can feel troubled; it happens that a person's faith can waver. What does one do then? One turns to God in prayer and implores God to help recapture one's true faith."

And Rebbe Pinhas understood that Moses had meant him too.

Though he was one of the closest and most striking companions of the Besht, Rebbe Pinhas never formally joined the Hasidic movement. As an elder statesman, he remained on the sidelines, watching with interest and amusement what was happening onstage.

After the death of the Founder, his peers wanted Rebbe Pinhas at one point to at least assume the role of mediator, to be an arbiter in the power struggle between the two factions, the two systems, that represented the two contenders: Rebbe Dov-Ber of Mezeritch and Rebbe Yaakov-Yosseph of Polnoye. But Rebbe Pinhas refused to take sides openly.

Actually, he himself would have made an excellent candidate to succeed the Besht. He was respected and celebrated by scholars and disciples alike. The Besht's affection for him was well known. Once the Besht was asked to give his opinion of his friends, and he did. When he came to Rebbe Pinhas he stopped: Rebbe Pinhas was an exception. The famous "Grandfather of Shpole" admired him—so did the legendary Reb Leib, son of Sarah, who called him "the brain of the world." Hasidism would say that the Besht left his knowledge to the Maggid of Mezeritch, his saintliness to Reb Mikhal of Zlotchev and his wisdom to Rebbe Pinhas of Koretz. In Hasidic literature, Rebbe Pinhas is called the Sage.

Withdrawn, reserved, modest, with individualistic tendencies, he refused to be crowned Rebbe. He held no court, proposed no doctrine, promised no miracles, established no dynasty, declined honors and privileges. He had five sons but only one disciple, Rebbe Raphael of Barshad, a former beadle and gravedigger whom he had pulled out of anonymity. When Rebbe Pinhas died, on his way to the Holy Land, he was succeeded by this disciple. That day a Tzaddik saw the widowed Shekhina at the Wailing Wall in Jerusalem.

Rebbe Pinhas: one of the most human, one of the most gracious and beautiful characters in the Hasidic gallery.

Who was he?

As is the case with most of his illustrious contemporaries, not much is known of Rebbe Pinhas' childhood and formative years. Born in 1728 in Shklov, into a poor rabbinic family, of ancestors who had died as martyrs of the faith, he studied Talmud and Kabbala; he also showed an unusual interest in exact sciences and philosophy.

He rarely spoke of his father. Instead, he frequently referred to his grandfather—also Reb Pinhas—who had made it his lifework to roam around Eastern Europe, seeking out Jewish converts to Christianity to bring them back to the fold.

Rebbe Pinhas married young and led an austere life. For a while he taught small children and was nicknamed "the dark teacher," perhaps because of his dark complexion, or because of his taste for solitude and meditation.

Unlike the Besht, he quickly gained a wide reputation as a rabbinic and mystical scholar. His teachings contain commentaries on the Bible, the Zohar, the Talmud, and even on the code of behavior, the *Shulkhan Arukh.*

Also unlike the Besht, it had been his wish to be able to stay in one place and do his work there—but he could not. He fled Shklov to avoid arrest and took refuge in Miropol (Vohlnia). From there he moved to Koretz, then to Ostraha, where he stayed until he left for the Holy Land in 1791, only to come to die in Shipitovke.

He was kind and generous. His wife once shouted at the housekeeper, and was admonished by her husband: "Please—please do not raise your voice at any human being; a human being is precious, so precious." He himself spoke softly, patiently. A devoted husband, a good father, he rarely got angry. "I do not think I succeeded in defeating vanity," he once remarked. "But I did succeed in putting anger into my pocket—only when I need it do I pull it out."

Contemplative by nature, he would look at a visitor and say nothing—thereby asking his visitor to look at him and say nothing. He prayed quietly, meditatively, shunning all visible demonstrations of ecstasy.

At the death of the Besht in 1760, Rebbe Pinhas was barely thirty-two, so he must have been quite young when they first met. The Besht treated him as an equal and went out of his way to win him over, although, unlike the Besht's other companions— such as Reb Gershon of Kitev, Reb Nahman of Kossov, and Reb Mikhal of Zlotchev—Rebbe Pinhas did not belong to an existing esoteric-ascetic group. He represented no potential ally, no influential clan whose adherence was important to the new movement. No, the Besht wanted Rebbe Pinhas for what he was and not for what he possessed; he wanted him for himself and not for the movement. Perhaps he needed him more as a friend than as a follower.

"Man is not alone," the Besht is supposed to have told him when they first met. "God makes us remember the past so as to break our solitude. Our forefathers stand behind us, some of them tested or chosen by God. Whatever they did, they did for us.

7

Whatever we do, we do for them. Long ago, in Egypt, every one of us strove for the preservation of the holy tongue, the names of our ancestors and their descendants, and the memory of the Covenant. Every one of us sat at the Prophets' feet to receive their teachings. Every one of us marched through the desert, to Sinai and from Sinai. Every one of us watched the splendor and desolation of Jerusalem. We all followed Reb Yohanan Ben-Zakkai into exile; we all shared his anguish and pride. And that is why we must stay together."

Clearly, there was something delicate, reticent and yet warm, in their relationship. Their mutual respect and affection went so far as to prevent the one from trying to change the other.

Legend has it that Rebbe Pinhas visited the Besht twice—and that the Besht visited him twice. Another Hasidic tradition claims that Rebbe Pinhas learned three things from the Besht; but it does not reveal what they were. In exchange, Rebbe Pinhas taught the Besht three things. Perhaps the same things.

The two friends evidently were together on the last Shavuoth when the Besht was lying on his deathbed. Most of the disciples had obeyed the Master's wish and returned home. Rebbe Pinhas stayed. At one point he began to pray, quietly but fervently, interceding with heaven on behalf of the old Master. "Too late," the Besht whispered, "too late, Pinhas. What is done is done; what is done will not be undone."

In the dispute over who was to be the Besht's successor, Rebbe Pinhas, characteristically, felt closer to the losers—in particular to the dead Master's son, Reb Tzvi-Hersh, whose name is frequently mentioned in his sayings. Rebbe Pinhas was Reb Tzvi-Hersh's understanding confidant and protector.

He also maintained cordial and even warm relations with Reb Yaakov-Yosseph of Polnoye, who had aspired to succeed the Besht after serving him faithfully, but who was not chosen. Feeling rejected and bitter, Reb Yaakov-Yosseph chose to celebrate Shabbat alone. Only Rebbe Pinhas kept him company—occasionally.

Once Rebbe Pinhas tried to console his unhappy friend with the following parable: "When the king retires at night, his crown rests on a nail fastened to the wall. Why on a nail, a common object used by common people for common purposes, and not on the head of a minister especially selected for such a distinct honor? I shall tell you why: after a while, with the crown on his head, the minister might take himself seriously. No such danger with a nail . . ."

From this we may deduce that there must have existed some tension in his relations with the winner, Rebbe Dov-Ber, the great Maggid of Mezeritch. Not that Rebbe Pinhas had objected to the Maggid's election, or that he lacked consideration for his virtues and talents. No, he had high regard for the new leader of the movement. But in his own gentle way, Pinhas distrusted all leaders. That is why he refused to become one himself. For a long time he wore no rabbinic garment, sat on no throne, and rejected all admirers. He would wear poor clothes, and sit with beggars and strangers near the stove, far from the limelight. Was it that he felt unworthy or unable of guiding others toward truth? Perhaps he worried too much about the perils of vanity inherent in leadership—was afraid of fame.

The famous Grandfather of Shpole told the following story: "For years and years I lived the life of a wanderer, in the company of beggars, going from town to town, from village to village. Once we happened to arrive in Koretz on Shabbat Eve. So we went to attend services conducted by Rebbe Pinhas. When the services were over, he greeted every one of us. When my turn came to shake his hand, he looked at me—and embraced me; he knew who I was. Years later, when I was no longer anonymous, I came to visit him again; the Grandfather of Shpole wished to pay his respects to the Tzaddik of Koretz. Again it was Shabbat Eve. Again Rebbe Pinhas greeted all the strangers. Then came my turn. He looked at me and said: 'Who are *you*? Where do *you* come from?'"

How typical of Rebbe Pinhas. When *nobody* knew the Grandfather of Shpole, he recognized him. When *everybody* knew him, he did not.

As for the Grandfather of Shpole, he concluded the story by saying: "It is not good to be famous, no, it is not good, I am telling you."

Among Rebbe Pinhas' numerous aphorisms, all reflecting common sense and wisdom, many relate to the pitfall of vanity. How to unmask it, how to fight it and vanquish it.

"If someone finds it necessary to honor me," he said, "that means he is more humble than I. Which means he is better and saintlier than I. Which means that I should honor him. But then, why is he honoring me?"

His disciple, Reb Raphael of Barshad, said: "When I shall appear before the heavenly tribunal, its members will question me on my various sins, and I, naturally, shall do my best to invent all kinds of excuses. Why didn't I study enough? I had neither the talent nor the time. Why didn't I pray with greater concentration? I was too busy making a living. And fasting, did I do some fasting? No, no, I was too weak. What about charity? No, no, I was too poor. But then they will ask me: 'If this is how it was—if you didn't study and didn't pray, if you lacked both compassion and charity, if you were too busy with yourself, how did it come about that you exuded such vanity?' And to this I shall have no answer, no excuse."

Rebbe Pinhas said: "Every sin is linked to a reason, good or bad—with the sole exception of vanity, which needs no reason to grow and grow. One can easily lie in rags on the ground and be hungry, empty of virtues and empty of knowledge, and still think endlessly: I am great, I am learned, I am just."

He also said: "Everything I know I learned before, sitting in the last row, out of sight. Now I am here, occupying a place of honor, and I don't understand . . ."

Of course, all Masters were aware of the spiritual threat inherent in their position. One cannot claim to possess powers without falling into the trap of believing that one deserves them. From the Maggid on, most Hasidic leaders stressed the absolute and constant need to fight pride and complacency. Except that he, Rebbe Pinhas, refused even to be tempted.

What, then, attracted him to Hasidism? Only the Besht and his friendship? No. He stayed attached to the movement some thirty years after the death of its Founder. His motives were not only of a personal nature; they were linked to the conditions inside the Jewish communities in Eastern Europe.

Hasidism was then the most revolutionary movement in Judaism. It excited the young, stimulated the dreamers, the poor, the desperate, the defeated. The most excellent came to join; this can be seen by the quality of the Besht's early companions. They were all great scholars of renown. They, too, had felt that Hasidism was accomplishing something vital and necessary for Jewish continuity: it was offering hope to the hopeless and a sense of belonging to those who needed it. The uprooted, isolated, impoverished, and uneducated villagers who, due to conditions not of their making, lived on the edge of history, and even outside its boundaries, suddenly felt linked to the people and the destiny of Israel. The force of the movement lay not in ideology but in life: the Besht literally changed the climate and the quality of Jewish life in hundreds and hundreds of towns and villages; his victories meant survival for their dispersed communities.

For those were cruel times for Eastern European Jewry. While Washington and his generals fought for American independence and the French revolutionaries proclaimed the reign of reason and liberty, Jews in Russia and Poland were alone and miserable. Polish Jews were still accused— regularly—of ritual murder. A Polish author wrote: "Just as freedom cannot be conceived without the right to protest, Jewish matzoth for Passover cannot be made without Christian blood . . ."

In Britain, Parliament rejected proposals granting civil rights to Jews . . . In Rome, Pope Pius VI

13

condemned seven thousand Jews, of his own city, to public disgrace . . . In Russia, Jews were persecuted and massacred . . . Voltaire and Rousseau, Kant and Goethe, Mozart and Goya, Danton and Robespierre—all were contemporaries of the Besht and the Maggid of Mezeritch and Rebbe Pinhas of Koretz, and it was as though they had nothing in common. Jewish history was removed from history. Jews were still relegated to subhuman status, not only by Christian fanatics but by enlightened secularists as well.

Thus the Jews had good reason to doubt society's wisdom and justice. They had good reason to doubt the absolute power of rationalism. So they turned inward and became mystical. They turned to the Rebbe, for only he knew how to comfort them, how to impart to them a sense of sacredness. Suddenly, and for the first time in centuries, they realized that they were not useless creatures. Every one of their gestures, every one of their prayers, no matter how awkward, counted and made a difference. The shepherd who played his recorder on Yom Kippur performed an action that had its reverberations in the highest spheres. The beggar's blessing compelled God to offer His own.

God is everywhere, said the Besht. In pain too? Yes, in pain too—especially in pain. God *is,* and that means that He dwells in every human being. In the unlearned too? Yes, in the unlearned too. In the sinner too. In the humble, in the humble most of all, He can be found. And He can be perceived by everyone. Sitting on His throne, said Rebbe Pinhas, He can be approached both through the tears of the penitent and the fervor of the worshiper. God *is,* God is *one;* and that means He is the same to people who turn to Him in different ways.

This offer of consolation was, at the same time, an appeal for unity. Within the Hasidic framework, Jews were told that they could fulfill themselves—as Jews—in more ways than one: the learned through their learning, the poor through their piety. God is not indifferent and man is not His enemy—this was the substance of the Hasidic message. It was a message against despair, against resignation; it sensitized the individual Jew to his own problems and made him aware of his ability to solve them. It taught him that hope must be derived from his own history, and joy from within his own condition.

Hasidism's concern for the wretched, for the victimized and forgotten Jew, induced many distinguished scholars to change their milieu, their way of life, and join the movement, and after the passing of the Maggid of Mezeritch, in 1772, they became its leaders. They responded to a need, hence their inevitable success.

Rebbe Pinhas, too, became popular, and resented it. Too many people visited him for too many reasons, taking too much of his time away from study and meditation. So one Yom Kippur he addressed this plea to God:

"Master of the Universe, forgive my audacity. I know I should thank You for the gifts You have bestowed upon me, thank You for being so liked by Your children. But do understand, please, that I have no time left for You. Do something, anything. Make people like me less . . ."

His wish was granted. People stopped visiting him at home, no longer greeted him on the street. And he was happy. But then came the Succoth holiday. As was the custom, he recited the *Oushpizin* prayer with true fervor, inviting the Shepherds of our people to enter the tent and be his guests. The first one to appear was Abraham; he stood at the entrance but refused to step inside, explaining: "If nobody comes to you, I must stay away too. A Jew must live with his people, not only for his people . . ." Next day Rebbe Pinhas addressed another plea to God. And became popular once more.

This, too, is part of the Hasidic message: there is a solution to loneliness—and loneliness is no solution. What is the significance of *Tikoun* (mystical reparation)? Rebbe Pinhas would ask. It is to be concerned not only with yourself but with everything that goes on around you; help others and you will help yourself. You want to serve God? Start with serving His children. Knowledge is to be shared, as is faith and everything else.

People brought him money, which he promptly distributed among the poor. Once he remarked: "I only desire what I already possess." How simple and how wise—better to desire what one has than to have what one desires.

Often students would turn to him for help in matters of faith. To one he said: "True, God may be hiding, but you know it. That ought to be sufficient." Will the student suffer less? No, he will suffer differently.

Having been told that atheists were demanding proof of God's existence, he rushed to the House of Study, opened the Holy Ark, seized the sacred scrolls and shouted: "I swear, I swear that God exists; isn't that proof enough?"

A student suffered from such anguish that he did not dare speak about it. Rebbe Pinhas looked at him and smiled: "I know, I know how you feel . . . but tell me, if *I* know, don't you think that *He* also knows?"

Speaking on grave and urgent topics, he would display a subtle sense of humor.

"All that is important is rare," he once remarked. "Millions and millions of people inhabit the earth, but only a few are Jewish. Among the Jews, only a few are learned. Among the learned, only a few are pious. And even fewer are those who know how to pray properly."

Another time: "God created Eve to serve as

Adam's *ezer kenegdo,* according to Scripture: to help him—against him. What does that mean? Well, imagine you visit a rich man, asking for charity. He welcomes you warmly and says: 'Oh, I wish I could, I so wish I could give as much as you need, as much as you deserve, but you see, I cannot; my wife is against it.' "

A student asked him: "What am I to do? I am pursued by evil temptations." And he answered: "Are you sure? Are you sure it is not the other way around?"

Perceptive and sharp-minded, Rebbe Pinhas was also naïve. He was convinced, for instance, that all sicknesses originate in lies: a person who does not lie cannot be ill. Also: When a Jew answers a question, he defeats the enemy of Israel; if his answer is correct, all his enemies are defeated. Also: When telling lies would be considered as grave a transgression as adultery, the Messiah would appear.

On Judgment Day, he would say, even the lectern will be judged, and sentenced to serve either for study or for feeding the stove.

Also: After his death a Tzaddik ascends from one degree to another, higher and higher, until he becomes first a sacred letter, then a sacred thought and finally a sacred name.

And this advice he loved to repeat in the name of the Besht: If you feel the urge to praise, praise God; if you feel the urge to blame, blame yourself.

. . .

Rebbe Pinhas' posthumously published book
—*Midrash Pinhas*—contains such aphorisms, parables, and insights, combining the written tradition
with the oral one, sealed secrets with revealed inten-
tions. He loved the Book of Splendor; he would
"take refuge in the Zohar."

Redemption occupied his thoughts and
dreams. What Hasid does not wait for the Messiah?
What Rebbe does not try to hasten his coming? To be
Jewish is to link one's fate to that of the Messiah—to
that of all those who are waiting for the Messiah.
How is one to accelerate events? Never mind the
Kabbalistic methods. They are too complicated, involved, and inaccessible; and then, they have not
proved too successful in the past. No, better try
simpler ways. Better appeal to simpler people.
Every person may change the course of history; it is
in the power of every individual to shorten exile.

Therein lies Rebbe Pinhas' originality. In his
teachings, he barely mentions the central role of the
Tzaddik, the Just Man, as mediator between heaven
and earth, as the instrument chosen by God to make
His will known and implemented. Instead he
stresses the importance of each individual, no matter how saintly or how ignorant. It is enough to
fulfill certain basic and practical commandments to
enable the Redeemer to appear in our midst for one
hour—to one other human being, and then to more
and more.

19

"If I so desired," said Rebbe Pinhas, "I could bring the Messiah as easily as I can lift a straw; but I prefer to rely on the Almighty. And He relies on man. If all Jews would give charity, redemption would occur."

On another occasion he said: "If all men would speak the truth, there would be no further need to bring the Messiah; he would be here already. Just as the Messiah brings truth, truth brings the Messiah." Truth: Rebbe Pinhas' total obsession and all-consuming passion.

"I broke all my bones while working on myself to attain truth," he said. "This lasted twenty-one years: seven years to discover what truth is; another seven years to expel falsehood from my being; and the last seven years to receive truth and live it."

Respect for truth was so profound among his friends and followers that they dared not repeat his comments for fear of misquoting him. His heir, Rebbe Raphael of Barshad, was once stopped in the street by a man who asked him: "Aren't you Reb Raphael of Barshad?"—"Yes . . . I think so," replied the Rebbe.

Summoned to testify on behalf of a man whose innocence he doubted, the same Rebbe Raphael spent all night weeping: he could not bring himself to tell a possible lie. He cried and cried. And died at dawn.

Once, during *Maariv* services, Rebbe Pinhas let out a cry so full of pain that his followers were anguished. The countess who owned Koretz happened to pass by his window just then. "I have never heard a cry filled with such truth," she told her escorts. When Rebbe Pinhas was informed of her comment, he smiled; he liked it. "Everybody can find truth," he remarked, "even Gentiles." On another occasion he emphasized: "We must love even the wicked among the Gentiles and pray for them; only then will redemption materialize."

But, of course, his main concern was for his own community—his own people—in whose behalf he pleaded with God Himself. "If only I knew how to sing," he once whispered, "I would force Him to come down and be with His children, witness their suffering, and save them." Another time he exclaimed: "Why do You leave Your people in exile? Why is it to last so long? Only because we did not—and do not—observe Your Law? But tell me, tell me, who compelled You to give it to us? Did we ask for it, did we want it? It was You who made us receive it . . . Furthermore, Master of the Universe, tell me: didn't You know even then that we would not comply with all Your laws? Still You chose us— then why are You angry?"

Like his celebrated contemporary Rebbe Levi-Yitzhak of Berditchev, he would speak to God on Yom Kippur—in Yiddish—and plead the cause of Israel with such strength and conviction that whoever heard him trembled with emotion.

Another passion that dominated Rebbe Pinhas' life was friendship.

Not only was he a friend to his peers and their Rebbes, but he was also a friend to his pupils; his role was forever that of a friend. He understood that Hasidism, in order to justify its ideals in human terms, would have to grow into a center that radiates friendship, which it did. *Dibouk Khaverim*—closeness among friends—was among Hasidism's cardinal precepts. People came to Mezeritch, and later to Lizensk, Rizhin, and Lublin, not only to see the Master but also to meet friends, share joys and sorrows, and help one another with a gesture, a word, a smile, a song, a tale.

Said Rebbe Raphael of Barshad: "Our Master and teacher Rebbe Pinhas of Koretz invited me once to join him in his coach. Unfortunately, there was not enough room. 'Do not worry,' our Master said reassuringly, 'Do not worry; let us be close friends and there will be room.' "

Rebbe Raphael also recalled: "Rebbe Pinhas loved to speak of friendship; often he referred to God, blessed-be-He and blessed-be-His-Name, as a friend, a true friend. And he would speak about this at length with a burning heart."

This tale alone would be sufficient to make us love and admire Rebbe Pinhas of Koretz. We have known God to be a father, a judge, a king; yet never did He seem to assume the role of friend to man, a role attributed to Him by Rebbe Pinhas alone.

Yet Rebbe Pinhas, who sought friendship in every person, everywhere, even in heaven, spent his last months on earth in sadness. Like most great Masters of that period, he somehow sank into melancholy—just what he desperately sought to avoid.

No definite facts about his change of mood and outlook are available. Only hints. And mainly intuitions. But intuition in Hasidic literature is as important and as revealing as elaborate statements by fervent followers.

An unexpected event took place in the year 1791—the last year of Rebbe Pinhas' life. Suddenly he left Ostraha, where he had served as rabbi, and went to Shipitovke to bid farewell to his father-in-law. His plan: to go and settle in the Holy Land. This was not the first time he felt the urge to go there. Years before, he had been tempted by the dream and had been about to set out on his journey. But he fell sick. "You do not want me to go," he said to God. "Good, I shall stay."

He stayed, but kept on dreaming. His love for Jerusalem was such that he tried to imagine it, but without success; it transcended his imagination. All he could do then was to imagine someone who had been in Jerusalem.

Now he was ready for the journey. He was determined to break with his familiar surroundings in Eastern Europe. And tear himself away from suffering in Diaspora.

The last years of his life were clouded by anxiety. He often spoke of unfulfilled wishes: "If only I could sing . . ." Or: "If only I could write down what my mouth is saying . . ." And also: "I am so afraid of being more wise than pious, but," he added cryptically, "I am too ill."

Often, too often, he was overwhelmed by gloom. "I study Zohar," he confided to Rebbe Raphael; "I explore its depth and sometimes I feel frightened. I sit there, staring at the Book of Splendor in front of me. I look and look and I keep silent—and that is all I do."

Once he revealed certain secrets to his companions—only to forbid them later to disclose them to others. Still later, he regretted having revealed them in the first place.

Reb Pinhas began to express himself strangely—recalling why he had been to Zaslav twenty-two years earlier. He said it was "to drive a certain great power" out of Poland . . . with his prayers. He wrote a mysterious letter to a mysterious Reb Yeshayahu who "had difficulties in *kabalat ol malkhut shamayim*—accepting the yoke of heaven."

He had become a changed man; perhaps he had been visited by some secret tragedy, some personal ordeal. What could it have been? What could have made him—the consoler—become so inconsolable?

His illness? His despair? Particularly over the state of affairs in the world and at home? Violent battles were raging between the Hasidim and their opponents, the Mitnagdim, who fought them with

Hasidic fervor and fanaticism. Excommunications, denunciations followed one another. Numerically the movement was blooming—in some thirty years it had conquered most of the forsaken communities in Eastern Europe—yet the possible spiritual decline represented a real danger. Suddenly there were too many schools, too many courts, too many Rebbes—and some of the followers had begun fighting among themselves. Clans were formed; sectarian loyalties were encouraged. These were still heroic times—with great Masters such as Rebbe Elimelekh of Lizensk, the Berditchever, and the Bratzlaver kindling flames everywhere. But the impetus and purity of the beginning were gone, or at least forgotten, in many quarters.

Rebbe Pinhas of Koretz must have been aware of all this. The attacks on Rebbe Nahman of Bratzlav. The dissension between Lizensk and Lublin. He must have gone through agony when he realized that Jews too—and even Hasidim—were capable of rejecting friendship. Jews too—and even Hasidim—could, on occasion, lack *Ahavat-Israel*. And he must have remembered the early days, the beauty of the Besht, the sobriety of the Maggid, the intensity of their disciples. He had witnessed three generations of leaders and followers. Did he foresee the deterioration of the movement? Was that the reason for his sadness? Or was it that, like the other Masters, he had heard too many tales of sorrow and pain? People were forever coming to him with their doubts and regrets, sharing with him their anguish and misery. Was it that, at one point, he could take it no more? Or was it that he had a premonition of what would be the end of Koretz?

The end occurred on Succoth, 1941. The Germans liquidated the ghetto. The last of its Jews disappeared in the tempest. Was it Reb Pinhas' tragic intuition, or tragic imagination, that induced him to set the example and move away—away from Gentile hate and Jewish laxity, away from quarreling factions and their leaders, away from unfulfilled dreams? Did he simply want to leave everything behind and go—go to the land of vision and prophecy, go to weep in Jerusalem over Jerusalem and for Jerusalem—and weep as one weeps only in Jerusalem?

But it was written that, like his good friend the Besht, he would die on his way—abroad.

In Shipitovke, shortly before he was to leave, he began trembling with fever. He lay in excruciating pain; his mind was on fire and he spoke only of death . . . with great anguish. He did not want to die—not then, not there. He was afraid to die alone, with no friends around him. He asked that his disciple Reb Raphael be called. When he came, the Master felt better. They talked and talked—and when they stopped talking, Reb Pinhas refused to address anyone else in the room. For two days he lay motionless and mute. Then he began calling for his old friend Reb Haim of Krasna, who was not there. On the following Shabbat his condition worsened; the end was near. Reb Pinhas was heard whispering: "Haim, Haim, my friend, my brother—come stay with me . . . I am afraid . . . Save me from the Angel of Death, Haim . . . If you stay with me, my friend, I won't die."

A rabbinical council, convened in emergency by Rabbi Shimshon of Shipitovke, authorized the dispatch of a special messenger to summon Reb Haim of Krasna, who was spending Shabbat in a nearby village. The messenger carried a letter dated *Hayom shabbat kodesh*—on this day of Shabbat. It was a race against time, a race against death.

Time won. Death won. Hasidism lost. When Reb Haim of Krasna arrived, it was too late. His friend already belonged to another world.

His mystery remains intact. We don't know what happened to him at the end of his life—we never will. He who was always composed, calm, serene—why was he possessed by such fear at the end? What had he glimpsed? What visions did he have—and about whom? What questions? What solutions did he oppose to what enigmas? Did he suddenly realize that Jews have no friends— anywhere? Or that the Messiah would be late in coming—much later than he had anticipated, much later than he had feared?

He died—and Koretz died with him. And now he has become a sacred letter, a fascinating tale, an evocative name: a key to wisdom and compassion.

His longing is our longing, his questions remain ours . . . and *we* must continue.

# Rebbe Barukh
# of Medzebozh

And it came to pass that one of the celebrated
Rebbe Barukh's disciples was caught in Satan's net. The poor man was following a dangerous
path leading to darkness: he read forbidden books,
played with perilous thoughts, and looked into
hidden areas which only the chosen may approach
with their gaze. He dwelled on the edge of the
abyss, tempted by damnation.

When his Master, Reb Barukh of Medzebozh,
learned about this, he felt sad, but told himself:
Well, the boy is young, he's gullible. Next time he
comes, I will talk to him; I will reprimand him and
bring him back to God. But the disciple kept him
waiting. And in the meantime, other rumors, in-
creasingly disquieting, reached the Master. The
disciple, he was told, had stopped praying; he had
stopped studying; he had stopped meeting members of the Hasidic community. In fact, he no longer
lived among Jews.

Overcome by his distress, the Master told himself: He will come to see me, he'll have to; and I shall be more severe than ever, more rigorous than ever, and he will be compelled to return to the fold. But the disciple continued to keep him waiting.

Finally, the Rebbe had no choice left. One morning he decided to go and see him. And without telling anyone, he left and went to another town, far away, and there confronted his disciple. And before the young man could collect his thoughts and utter a word, the Rebbe spoke to him:

"You are surprised to see me here, in your room? You shouldn't be. I can read your thoughts, I know your innermost secrets. You are alone and trying to deepen your loneliness. You have already passed through, one after the other, the fifty gates of knowledge and doubt—and I know how you did it.

"You began with one question; you explored it in depth to discover the first answer, which allowed you to open the first gate; you crossed it and found yourself confronted by a new question. You worked on its solution and found the second gate. And the third. And the fourth and the tenth; one leads to the other, one is a key to the other. And now you stand before the fiftieth gate.

"Look: it is open. And you are frightened, aren't you? The open gate fills you with fear, because if you pass through it, you will face a question to which there is no answer—no human answer. And if you try, you will fall. Into the abyss. And you will be lost. Forever. You didn't know that. Only I did. But now you also know."

"What am I to do?" cried the disciple, terrified. "What can I do? Go back? To the beginning? Back to the first gate?"—"Impossible," said the Master. "Man can never go back; it is too late. What is done cannot be undone."

There was a long silence. Suddenly the young disciple began to tremble violently. "Please, Rebbe," he cried, "help me. Protect me. What is there left for me to do? Where can I go from here?"—"Look," said Rebbe Barukh. "Look in front of you. Look beyond that gate. What keeps man from running, dashing over its threshold? What keeps man from falling? Faith. Yes, son: beyond the fiftieth gate there is not only the abyss but also faith—and they are one next to the other . . ."

And the Rebbe brought his disciple back to his people—and himself.

This story is not characteristic of Rebbe Barukh; he would have found it undignified to pursue a recalcitrant pupil. He wanted people to come to him, to visit his palace, and pay him due homage. Why, then, did he make an exception? In matters of *pikuakh nefesh*—when a soul is in danger and in need of rescue—all rules are to be discarded. However, the way Rebbe Barukh dealt with the case is no less perplexing: he spoke of faith to someone whose problem was precisely that he had no faith.

A strange man, Rebbe Barukh of Medzebozh—one of the strangest among the Hasidic Masters of his time: he introduced anger into Hasidism.

Like his grandfather, the Besht, whom he was
eager to resemble, Rebbe Barukh did not fare well
with historians. Graetz vilified the first and Dubnov
downgraded the latter. Both judgments are un-
founded and unfair.

Like the Besht, Rebbe Barukh inspired passionate attitudes in friends and opponents alike.
Simple Hasidim were loyal to him; so were some,
only some, of their leaders.

Rebbe Israel of Rizhin declared: "In his presence a pious man became more pious, a wise man
grew wiser, and an imbecile more stupid."

Rebbe Zvi-Hersh of Ziditchoiv desired so
much to hear Rebbe Barukh sing the Song of Songs
that he hid in his study. Later he confided to friends:
"The Master was in ecstasy, his entire being aflame,
evolving in another world; and when he came to the
verse *Ani ledodi*—'I belong to my beloved as my
beloved belongs to me'—he repeated each word
with such fervor that I, too, found myself thrust into
another world."

Yet how is one to explain his taste for power,
his thirst for authority? The Besht did not wish to
impress anyone and impressed everyone; his
grandson also impressed his followers—only he
*wished* to impress them. Their personalities were
different and so were their life styles. The Besht was

constantly traveling; his grandson held court in his palace. The Besht was poor; his grandson was not. The Besht spent himself in efforts to spread joy; his grandson struggled with melancholy. The Besht spoke softly; his grandson shouted.

No wonder Rebbe Barukh was criticized, not only by opponents of the movement but also by some of its leaders. Some disagreed with his precepts, others with his methods. Too sensitive and self-centered, he resented the slightest sign of deviation or dissension. He considered himself the only ruler—the keeper of the Hasidic flame.

There were those who objected, but rarely in public. Celebrated Masters—such as Rebbe Levi-Yitzhak of Berditchev, the Seer of Lublin, the Rizhiner, Rebbe Shneur-Zalmen of Ladi—often came to spend Shabbat under his roof. Thanks to him, Medzebozh became a capital for the second time, attracting Hasidim from all over the Beshtian provinces. Medzebozh, the small village in Podolia, again became a center for pilgrimage, a glorious symbol of a glorious kingdom.

Appropriately, Rebbe Barukh's story is linked to a legend—a legend about his mother, who, as we all remember, has a special place in Hasidic literature.

The Besht had two children: Reb Tzvi-Hersh and his sister Oudil. They were totally different in character and temperament. Reb Tzvi-Hersh was shy, forlorn, unassuming, withdrawn—unable and unwilling to assure his father's succession at the head of the rapidly expanding movement.

His sister, on the other hand, was an extrovert. No woman is as romanticized, as admired in Hasidism, as she was. She brought to the movement an added dimension of youth and charm.

Oudil—the name is probably taken from Adèle, Adella—was honored by Hasidim as though she were a Rebbe herself. And, in a way, she was. At her father's side—always. Full of life, ideas, projects; forever in the middle of events, forever generating excitement, enthusiasm; forever in the middle of a story. Hasidim believed that the Shekhina rested on her face.

Married to Reb Yehiel Ashkenazi, she managed to take care of him—of their grocery store, of their two sons, and her father. When the Besht was sick, she was at his bedside. There existed a special friendship, a singular complicity between the two. One has the feeling that he was closer to her than to his own wife—her mother.

She often accompanied the Besht in his travels, something her brother—or her mother—rarely did. Oudil seemed to be everywhere—never disturbing, never embarrassing; on the contrary, she made herself welcome, she made people feel good. She participated in the extraordinary adventure which her father had begun; and her father, lovingly, encouraged her to participate more and more, even when the Besht and his disciples went on their frequent retreats. When they prayed, when they conducted their mystical gatherings, when they celebrated, she was nearby. Oudil: the feminine grace, the humorous beauty of the Hasidic movement.

One evening she was present at a celebration. Her father's disciples sang and danced for hours and hours on end, aiming to achieve communion with God, trying to let their souls enter His. They chanted with fervor, they danced with exuberance—until they left behind all links with things earthly. They forgot their own senses; shoulder against shoulder, hand in hand, their eyes closed, they formed a circle of friendship, a circle around God and His people.

Oudil was looking at them, finding it breathtakingly beautiful, when suddenly she noticed that one disciple was losing his balance. His shoes had disintegrated, and sad, distressed, he had to leave his friends.

"Poor young man," Oudil said to her father.

The Besht smiled: "Promise him a pair of new shoes, if he promises you another son."

Both did. And thus, for the price of a pair of shoes, Oudil got her second son, Barukh. Tradition has it that she wanted him—and only him. She had given birth to one son already, Rebbe Ephraim, the future author and scholar—but Oudil wanted a Rebbe, not a writer. And so she had Reb Barukh.

What do we know about him? Much—but not too much. As we consult Hasidic sources, we cannot help but detect a certain reticence toward him. Few books are devoted to him; and his place in other Masters' legends is surprisingly modest. One could say that there he is known only by the hostility he aroused. They found him quarrelsome, arrogant, moody, and would have preferred not to deal with him. But how could they avoid it? He was the Besht's grandson and his impact on Hasidism could not be denied.

Born in 1757, he was three or four when his grandfather died. He grew up in the house of the Maggid of Mezeritch, and studied with Rebbe Pinhas of Koretz. He married into a wealthy family, lived first in Tultchin, then moved to Medzebozh, where he died at fifty-four.

He must have been a precocious child, and the Besht loved him.

A legend: A disciple asked the Besht the following question. Scripture tells us that "Abraham lifted his eyes and saw three men before him." The Zohar's comment is that the three men were our patriarchs: Abraham, Isaac and Jacob. How was it possible? wondered the disciple. How could Abraham have seen . . . Abraham?

The question was pertinent, and the Besht was about to answer it when his grandson, little Barukh, remarked: "What a foolish question! The Zohar does not speak about people but about symbols—and our three patriarchs symbolize God's attributes: grace, power, and magnificence."

True or not, we don't know—but the story could have been true. Reb Barukh followed in the footsteps of the child who spoke his mind, treated an anonymous disciple as though he were his own bad pupil, and who, in the presence of the Besht, dared speak of the Zohar at the age of three.

Little Barukh loved his grandfather, and spoke of him more than of his own father or mother. Tradition has it that Rebbe Pinhas of Koretz saw the small boy weeping over the passing of the Besht—and that *this* moved him more than the tragic event itself.

He studied with Rebbe Pinhas, but failed to learn his concept of wealth. Rebbe Pinhas used to say: "What shall I leave my children when I die? All the monies that my Hasidim *wanted* to give me—and I refused to accept." As for Rebbe Barukh, he accepted. Unlike Rebbe Pinhas, unlike his own elder brother, Reb Ephraim, he seems to have had an attachment for earthly possessions.

Once he felt the need to explain why he accepted money from his followers: "Imagine you must go and see the king. But the king is in one place and you are in another. The king is in his palace, inaccessible, surrounded by walls and fences, with guards standing at the gates. What do you do? You bribe the guards. You begin with those standing on watch outside, then you make your way inside. Naturally, the closer you come to the king, the more important the guards—and the higher the bribes. Well," he said, "Tzaddikim are keepers of the gate; they can be bribed."

Having married a rich girl, he could afford to study—but did not. His two brothers-in-law, both pious and learned men, were irritated by his behavior: whenever they studied, he slept; whenever they slept, he played games. So annoyed were they that they complained to their common father-in-law, who decided to take them all to Mezeritch. In the coach, Reb Barukh was humiliated by his companions: they made him sit next to the coachman. However, on the way back he had the best seat. For the Maggid of Mezeritch had told his angry visitors: "Leave Barukh alone; he knows what he is doing, and so do I. His games are serious—*if* you know how to read them. I know and so does he. And so does God."

With the Maggid as protector and the Besht as grandfather, Reb Barukh could not fail. He was

treated as a prince by Hasidic Masters and followers, whom he touched with his youth, his
exuberance—and his memories of the Besht.

When he became Rebbe, he went first to
Tultchin. Why Tultchin? Because of *its* memories.
Tultchin had been the scene of unspeakable mas-
sacres during the Khmelnitzki uprisings. Reb
Barukh wished to live there. Yet he did not stay there
long. Was it *because* of the memories? Or was it
because of the Mitnagdim, the opponents of
Hasidism, who made his life miserable with constant attacks and slanders?

He left for Medzebozh, his grandfather's capital. Why there? Probably because there he had nothing to fear from Mitnagdim. And also, because of
the name. Medzebozh would now be linked not
only to the Besht's name, but to his own as well.

From visitors, disciples, and chroniclers we
know much about his life there. His home was not
really a palace in our terms, but it was in theirs. He
had *gaboim* and *shamoshim*, secretaries and servants,
and displayed his riches especially on Shabbat and
during holidays.

He had children, whom he loved—an ailing
daughter, whom he loved even more. When
needed, he would personally travel to the big city
for medications for her.

In his home, as in that of his grandfather,
women were not relegated to the kitchen or to se-

cluded chambers. Was it Oudil's influence? In Medzebozh they participated in festive meals and sat together with distinguished guests—something the holy Seer of Lublin objected to rather violently. Their dispute, at least in the beginning, was due to feminine presence. When the holy Seer was invited to Reb Barukh's Shabbat table, he was shocked to find there the Master's wife and daughters. Worse: they took part in the conversation.

An episode: One day, as Rebbe Barukh was saying grace, repeating three times the verse *Vena al tatzrikheni adoshem elokenu lo lidey matnat basar vedam*—"May I not be dependent on other people's gifts"—his daughter Reisele interrupted him: "But, Father," she said, "isn't that your livelihood? You wish God to stop people from offering you money?" Answered Rebbe Barukh: "Only God gives—but He uses messengers."

He enjoyed having guests, entertaining them with stories, parables and songs. Before a fast he would offer them candy. A symbolic gesture: yes, there are reasons for us to mortify ourselves, but sweetness too is part of life and willed by God.

Once he was surprised by Reb Moshe of Ludmir while he was quarreling with his wife. "Do not worry," he told the visitor, "it is just like the Almighty disagreeing with the Shekhina, His divine presence—it is all for the sake of *Tikoun*, it is all meant to correct creation and shorten exile."

It was in Medzebozh that melancholy took

hold of Rebbe Barukh, though we do not know what provoked it nor when it was first noticed. All we know is that it invaded him one day—and that it remained unexplained. How could anyone teach the Hasidic idea and not receive its message of joy? How could one claim to continue the Besht's mission and yield to sadness? How could Rebbe Barukh be a Hasidic Master and look at creation with anger?

Is this why he met such hostility among his peers—because he did not conform to the traditional Beshtian concept of the Tzaddik, whose task is to guide and console, and serve as an example? Rebbe Barukh differed from most in many ways, and perhaps in all ways.

To begin with, he claimed to be their superior—no, more than that: their overseer. "Rebbe Barukh is climbing to heaven . . . on our heads," said Reb Sholem, the Maggid of Mezeritch's grandson.

True, Rebbe Barukh belittled other Hasidic Masters. He alone could dispose of the Besht's heritage, he maintained; he alone could spread it to Jewish communities in Podolia and beyond, if possible.

Modesty was not his most pronounced virtue. "My soul," he remarked, "knows its way in Torah, all gates are open to me." Once he told of a dream he had had: "A number of Masters and scholars were sitting around the table presided over by Rabbi Shimon bar-Yohai, who planted the fear of heaven in our hearts for not serving God as we should. We all began shivering. Then Rabbi Shimon bar-Yohai noticed me. He rose and came over to me and placed his hand on my shoulder. 'Barukh,' he said gently, 'you need not worry, I do not mean you—you are perfect.' " Another time Rebbe Barukh was seen pressing the Zohar to his heart, saying: "Rabbi Shimon bar-Yohai, I know you, and you know me."

At the same time, he liked to boast about his humility. Said he: "If there were a thousand humble men in this world, I am one of them; if there are only two, I am one of them."

Small wonder that some of his peers disliked him. He quarreled with most of them—he even had a dispute with the great Rebbe Shneur-Zalmen of Ladi, the founder of Chabad, who dared collect funds for ransoming prisoners—in Reb Barukh's domain, in Tultchin. "But it is an emergency," Reb Shneur-Zalmen argued, "we must save those Jews!"—"If you are a Tzaddik," Reb Barukh replied, "save them with prayers, not with money."

He was opposed even by his nephew, Rebbe Nahman of Bratzlav, who had enough enemies of his own. Few Rebbes disputed or even challenged Rebbe Barukh's greatness, but they were irked by it and one easily understands why: he disputed *their* greatness.

There was another reason too. In those years disciples of the great Maggid of Mezeritch were already at work inside hundreds of dispersed communities between the Dnieper and the Carpathian Mountains, revolutionizing Jewish life everywhere. They addressed themselves to forlorn and forsaken villagers in their own language, sharing their burdens and misery, turning imagination into a vehicle to take them away from misfortune; a small barrack was made into a sanctuary, and simple words into litanies. These new Masters were successful because they lived *with* their followers, helping them vanquish poverty through faith and faith alone. Only one Rebbe wanted to be different. And was.

Like the Rizhiner somewhat later, Reb Barukh dressed like a prince, behaved like a prince, expressed himself like a prince. He was the first Rebbe to introduce the external trappings of power and privilege into Hasidic lore. He was the first to stress the element of *malkhut*, of royalty, in the Tzaddik's role. His meals had to be royal feasts, his home a royal court.

A story: One day Reb Barukh visited his brother, Reb Ephraim and saw the poverty of his home—he had candlesticks made of clay and not of silver. "Do not be sad," said Rebbe Ephraim, "the light is the same." Shortly afterward, Reb Barukh offered his brother a set of silver candlesticks. But when he came to visit him again, they were not to be seen.

"Where are they?" he wanted to know.

"At the pawnbroker's," said Reb Ephraim, "I needed money."

"And it doesn't bother you?" asked Reb Barukh.

"No," said his brother. "I'll tell you why. I prefer to be at home and have my silverware elsewhere—than the other way around."

A hint of criticism? Maybe, though it would seem out of character. Reb Ephraim, the elder brother, was a gentle, sweet, unassuming man who never offended anyone—and would never have sought to pain his brother. So humble was Reb Ephraim that in his important book, *Degel machnei ephraim*, he is content with quoting the Besht and his immediate disciples and almost never speaks on his own behalf. Still, Reb Barukh must have envied him, for he once remarked: "I have not written a book—thank God for that."

He was suspicious both of the written word and the oral word. He was suspicious—period.

As he grew older, he became restless, moody; he felt a stranger everywhere—even in his own home. Uprooted, alienated, the king in him felt threatened. His obsession was that all men are strangers in the world. And that God too, in exile, dwells as a stranger in His own creation. One day he told his disciples: "Imagine someone who has been expelled from his country. He arrives at a place where he has no friends, no relatives; and the customs and the tongue of the land are unfamiliar to him. Naturally, he feels lonely, terribly lonely. Suddenly he sees another stranger who, like him, has no one to turn to—no place to go. The two strangers meet and become acquainted. They talk, and for a while walk the streets together. With some measure of luck, they may even become good friends. This is true of God and man; they are two strangers who try to become friends."

What a depressing concept of man and his relation to God! No wonder that many Masters rejected it—and him. They could have fought him publicly on these grounds alone. Why didn't they? Out of respect for his grandfather? Yes, but they respected the grandson as well. There was something charismatic about him. They may not have agreed with his methods, but they could not but recognize his genuine qualities of leadership. Also, they were afraid. Afraid of his somber gaze, afraid of his dark outbursts of anger.

This became his particular sign, his distinction: anger. The ability to be harsh, just as his peers were gentle. They blessed their followers; he insulted his. They sought to appease; he to annoy. However, his followers were not to be discouraged; they clung to him even more. They believed that the angrier he was, the kinder he was. They took his curses for benedictions—which only made him angrier.

Forever misunderstood, he tormented others, and himself. Why? Because of what was happening in the world, to the world? International politics left him indifferent. He did not mix into the affairs of Napoleon and the Czar, and expected no interference in his. Because, of what was then taking place inside the Jewish world? Possibly. The war between Hasidim and their opponents surely affected him. But what interested him most was what was going on inside the Hasidic universe.

Like his grandfather, Rebbe Barukh understood that in order to improve the world, one has to improve oneself first. If God does not dwell in me, whose fault is it? Have I prepared for Him a dwelling place worthy of His glory?

Often Reb Barukh was beset by doubts. The Besht was so great, so intense, so unique—and he, Reb Barukh, was his successor. Worse: the Besht was so majestic—and others pretended to be *his* successors. How could he keep calm? Strange: the grandson's way differed so much from his grandfather's. Is this how the Besht would have wanted his grandson to lead his community? With anger? In sadness?

One does not understand. No one seems to have tried to understand. No attempt was made to explain his bizarre outbursts, his depressions. People chose to move away from him, rather than criticize him or judge him. Perhaps they did not dare antagonize the grandson of the Besht, the son of Oudil, a Master who every morning wore the Besht's tephillin.

And again, we must insist: he was a man of greatness. He had an intense inner life; he was endowed with a burning vision. He could have led a peaceful life filled with honors, yet he chose to reject the safe course of preserving a glorious heritage and, instead, walked the perilous new path of self-interrogation. As the Besht's grandson, he could have kept what was given to him, yet he chose to risk everything and antagonize everybody! He detested the serene existence of the Tzaddik. He rebelled all the time, without really knowing against whom or what. And there we find him poignantly human—sublime and stimulating. Listen:

Rabbi Moshe of Savran came to spend Shabbat in Medzebozh. After services, Reb Barukh paced up and down the room, singing *"Shalom aleikhem,"* welcoming the angels of peace who bring the light of Shabbat and its serenity on their wings; then he recited with his customary fervor the prayer *Ribon kol haolamim*—"Thank You, Master of the Universe, for Your generous gifts—those I have received and those yet to come . . ." Suddenly he stopped and

47

said in a loud voice: "Why am I thanking You now for gifts to come?" He repeated the question several times, and after a long silence, began to weep.

"Why is the Rebbe crying?" wondered Rebbe Moshe of Savran. "Because of the question?"

"Yes," said Rebbe Barukh.

"And . . . the answer? What is the answer?" asked the disciple.

"Here it is," said Rebbe Barukh. "We thank Him now for gifts to come—in case we will not be able to do so when we receive them." And again he began to weep.

"Why is the Rebbe crying?" asked the disciple once more. "Because of the answer?"

"Yes," said Rebbe Barukh, "because of the answer. I think of the future, which, God willing, may prove to be good to me—but what if I will be unable to give God my gratitude? How could I live without gratitude?"

Later he added: "You see, the question is good—and so is the answer. And both make me cry."

But on another Shabbat, when he had a visitor from Jerusalem as his guest, he looked at him for a long while and asked: "Are you sad?"

"Yes," said the guest, "I am; I cannot help it, I have traveled too much, I have seen too much, lived too much."

"But it's Shabbat, my friend! You are not traveling now, you are witnessing no suffering!"

"But I do," said the guest.

"Then I order you to shake your sadness
away!" And after a silence, he added: "Come, I'll
teach you."

One of his sayings: God and man's love of God
are alike—for they are boundless.

Another one: People are careful not to swallow
live ants but are ready to eat up their fellow men.

Also: Every person is a vessel taking into itself
whatever its owner pours into it: wine or vinegar.

The world looks brightly illuminated, he said,
for those who don't want it—and gloomy and dark
to those who seek to possess it.

He also said: I am afraid of Cossacks—one is
enough to scare me. Ten would scare me even
more—and a thousand, a thousand times more.
And yet, they scare me less than the tiniest of sins
that I could commit.

"Say something," pleaded the holy Seer of
Lublin during their memorable encounter. "I am
told everywhere that you talk so well. Please,

Rebbe. Talk. Say something, anything. I would so
like to take your words with me—even one. You talk
so well—couldn't you talk to me?"

"No," said Rebbe Barukh. "I would rather be
mute than talk well."

Rebbe Levi-Yitzhak of Berditchev, who loved
peace—and to make peace—managed nevertheless
to appear on Reb Barukh's blacklist.

Perhaps it had to do with the fact that Reb
Levi-Yitzhak had sent two emissaries to report on
Reb Barukh's life style: Did he study Talmud? And
observe all the laws of Torah? Was it true that he read
other people's thoughts?

The emissaries brought back their report, and
the answer was yes to all three questions. Yes,
Reb Barukh could read other people's secret
thoughts—and he proved it. He told the emissaries:
"Go and tell the Rebbe of Berditchev that God sees
and forgives; not I—I see and don't forgive."

Actually, this was not true: Reb Barukh forgave
Reb Levi-Yitzhak. The two Masters had nothing but
affection and esteem for one another. And a beadle
in Berditchev could confirm and corroborate it.

Listen: Reb Barukh was told of a certain Mitnagged in Berditchev who, unfortunately, happened to be a good scholar; so he used his
scholarship, naturally, to make Reb Levi-Yitzhak's
life miserable. He' would interrupt his lectures,

ridicule his sermons—in short: he was unbearable as only some erudite Mitnagdim can be.

"Let him come to see me, and thereafter he will keep quiet," said Reb Barukh.

Somebody informed the Mitnagged, who repeated it in public. "Good," he said insolently, "I shall go and see him. Who is he? What is he? What is his strong point?—"The Zohar," he was told.— "Good," he said. And he began studying the Zohar page after page, chapter after chapter, with commentaries and commentaries on commentaries— until one day he felt he was ready. And he went to Medzebozh—equipped with a difficult passage of the Zohar intended for Reb Barukh, expecting to trap him right away. To his surprise, he found the Master reading the Zohar, opened on the very page he had meant to open for him.

"You seem astonished," said the Rebbe. "What puzzles you: that I study Zohar—or that I made *you* study Zohar?" And without allowing the Mitnagged to reply, he continued: "Usually you study Talmud, right?"—"Right."—"And you know it?"— "Yes," said the visitor.

And the Rebbe told this story: "Do you know the legend about the light that shines above the child's head before he is born? This light enables him to study and absorb the entire Torah. But one second before he enters into the world, the child receives a slap from his personal angel; in his fright, he forgets all that he has learned. Well, there is

something in this legend that one fails to understand. Why study if it is all to be forgotten? Do you
know the answer?"

The visitor remained mute.

"No?" said the Rebbe. "Let me explain it to
you. It is to teach man the importance of
forgetfulness—for it, too, is given by God. If man
were not to forget certain things, if he were to remember the time that passes and the approaching
death, he would not be able to live as a man among
men. He would no longer go to plow his field, he
would no longer build a house; nor would he have
children. That is why the angel planted forgetfulness in him: to allow him to live. But tell me, what
happens when the angel forgets . . . to make you
forget?" Rebbe Barukh looked at his visitor and
waited before continuing: "If he forgot—I can still
do it for him."

And because the erudite Mitnagged had used
knowledge against his fellow men, the Rebbe
punished him. The Mitnagged forgot all that he had
ever known and became a simple beadle in the
synagogue—where Reb Levi-Yitzhak could, from
then on, speak and lecture without fear of being
disturbed or interrupted.

Another story:
Rebbe Barukh's grandson, Yehiel, came running into his study, all in tears.

"Yehiel, Yehiel, why are you crying?"

"My friend cheats! It's unfair; he left me all by myself, that's why I am crying."

"Would you like to tell me about it?"

"Certainly, Grandfather. We played hide-and-seek, and it was my turn to hide and his turn to look for me. But I hid so well that he couldn't find me. So he gave up; he stopped looking. And that's unfair."

Rebbe Barukh began to caress Yehiel's face, and tears welled up in his eyes. "God too, Yehiel," he whispered softly, " . . . God too is unhappy; He is hiding and man is not looking for Him. Do you understand, Yehiel? God is hiding and man is not even searching for Him . . ."

Weeping over God and man alike, Rebbe Barukh could not help but sink into melancholy. Like other Hasidic Masters before him and after him, he knew that the secret of redemption lies in the union between Creator and creation. But what if Creator and creation were to remain strangers forever? Reb Barukh's despair was of an existential nature. Divine severity frightened him less than divine separation. Let God be our king, our father, or even our judge—but let Him not be estranged from us!

Perhaps that was the secret of Reb Barukh's anguish and anger: And what if I was wrong? And what if, due to man's foolishness, God were to hide His face forever? And what if the Besht and his allies were powerless to bring God and man closer together? And what if they were unable to protect the people of Israel from new and old dangers? And if the Besht was powerless—what could his grandson do? What hopes were left for him?

People came to him with pleas for heavenly intercession, with pleas for miracles—and he replied with outbursts of rage: he was against miracles. When Prophet Elijah performed miracles on Mount Carmel, the people shouted: *"Adoshem hu haelohim*—Look! God is God." Said Rebbe Barukh: "The Prophet was great and so were the people, for they didn't shout: 'Look! Miracles, miracles.' But . . . 'Look! God is God.' They disregarded the miracles."

But his followers wanted miracles. What could he have done? Levi-Yitzhak of Berditchev chose to side *with* his people—against the Almighty. Not Reb Barukh. Hence his rage—at himself, at the situation in which he found himself. At his followers, who forced him to choose. Rage at his peers—to provoke *their* anger. Yes, he wanted them to be angry, and to begin by being angry with him.

Then he knew melancholy. Sadness. Despair. So great was his suffering that a famous jester, a *shokhet* named Hershele Ostropoler, had to be engaged to cheer him up. Poor, penniless, Hershele had a biting sense of humor. That's why he was forever leaving positions; he would invariably antagonize his communal employers. Hundreds of stories circulated about his sharp tongue and quick mind.

Once his wife complained: "The children have nothing to eat; go get them some bread." Hershele went to the marketplace with a whip in his hand, shouting: "Who wants to go to Zhitomir for half the price?" So some people, to save half the fare, flocked to him instead of taking the coach. He made them pay, and then said: "Follow me." He led them out of town, and farther. Midway, the "passengers" asked him: "Hershele, where are the horses?"

"Who spoke of horses?" he said. "I spoke of half fare . . ."

Later he told his wife: "See? the important thing is to have a whip—if you have one, horses will come to you anyway . . ."

One night he was awakened by his wife: "Hershele, listen! Thieves! There are thieves in the house."—"Really?" said Hershele. "If they find anything valuable, then *we* are lucky . . ."

One evening Reb Barukh told Hershele to light the candles, for it was dark in the room. The jester lit one candle. "Hershele," scolded the Rebbe, "one candle is not enough, I cannot see!" Next day Hershele lit more than one, more than ten, more than thirty—he wasn't going to stop lighting candles. "Hershele, Hershele," scolded the old Rebbe again. "Are you going to blind me now?"

"I don't understand," said the jester. "Yesterday you were against darkness, now you are against light."

And Reb Barukh burst out laughing. "Hershele," he said, "you want to teach *me* when to be angry?"

With his stories and witty aphorisms, Hershele made him laugh—and be angry too. For Hershele was irreverent, in the classic manner of jesters, and told the Rebbe things that he didn't like to hear. So much so that at least one Hasidic source maintains that on one occasion Hershele went too far . . . and the Rebbe grew too angry . . . and so the Rebbe ordered his followers to throw the jester out. And Hershele, broken and sick, never returned.

Hershele, too, was a tragic figure—as tragic and as secretive as his Master. Whatever it was the Rebbe wanted to achieve with anger, Hershele tried to achieve with laughter.

Again and again we stumble upon this word, "anger." It dominated the Rebbe's last years. Once he explained his behavior, pointing to the Zohar, which speaks of a certain anger that is blessed from above and below, and it is named: Barukh. At his deathbed his followers found the Zohar opened on that very page.

He tried to explain—others did not. They did not even seem to mind. Do we? No, not really. We try to understand him, and love him. Others forgave his taste for luxury and power; we forgive his anger. Perhaps he wanted to teach us something about the Tzaddik, namely: that though the Tzaddik must be revered and feared, he must also be measured in human terms. The Tzaddik is human—and must be. No true greatness, no real holiness can be attained if it is at the expense of one's humanity. To deny one's weaknesses is but another weakness. The Tzaddik is no angel, no heavenly saint—the Tzaddik is simply more human than his followers, and that is why he is their leader.

Of course, that idea was elaborated on by the Besht, but Reb Barukh perfected it. The Besht said: "Once upon a time we tried to come closer to God through study, prayer, fasting, mortification and contemplation—but I intend to open a new way which will enable man to approach God through love: love of God, love of Torah and love of Israel."

Perhaps his grandson, Reb Barukh, understood all of a sudden that love alone—in a world without love, filled with violence and crowded with strangers—is not enough to assure the survival of his people . . . Perhaps he thought that a certain measure of anger, of rage, was necessary for the people of Israel . . . Hence his sadness, hence his despair: how can one not despair of a world where rage is needed for redemption?

The key to his enigma may possibly be found in his excessive passion for *Shir-hashirim,* the Song of Songs. What is the Song of Songs? A love song? Of course—a sublime chant of love. But what kind of love? Unhappy love, heavy with melancholy and nostalgia. It is a song of endless waiting and faithfulness, it is majestic and moving but marked by tragedy: the couple remains separated, torn apart. God waits for Israel while Israel is waiting for God, who is looking for His Shekhina, who is following Israel, who suffers with God, and at times for God, and always because of God.

And yet—beyond sadness, beyond despair, there *is* love, and there always will be. Without such love, which forever calls for its own transcendence, man's life would not be less tragic but less lofty and therefore empty and pointless.

A romantic idea? Never mind. Aren't we at the beginning of the nineteenth century, on the threshold of the Romantic movement, with its agonies and dreams, its tears and outcries?

Rebbe Barukh died in 1811—leaving us his Song of Songs, but not his rage. Perhaps it was but a mask—one that both revealed and obscured his passionate love for his people.

The more you study his sayings, his stories, his life, the more you discover beauty in the man himself. Suddenly you realize that more than his contemporaries—or ours—he grasped the awesome weight of questions. More than his peers—

and ours—he understood that one must never avoid questions, as one must not turn one's gaze away from the abyss. Remember the story we told at the beginning? One must go through the gates. And confront truth face to face. And look into the eyes of despair—and never mind if you will remain prisoner of your own anguish. Alone . . . you probably will remain prisoner. So . . . don't be alone. A Hasid is never alone, even if the Tzaddik is.

The beauty of Rebbe Barukh is that he could speak of faith not as opposed to anguish but as being part of it. "Faith and the abyss are next to one another," he told his disciple. "I would even say: one within the other. True faith lies beyond questions; true faith comes after it has been challenged."

In conclusion, we have learned from his tales that love and anger are compatible, provided they are motivated by *Ahavat-Israel,* by concern for Israel.

Granted, we are all strangers under the sun. Granted, God's ways are not always understandable—or bearable. Is that a reason for us to leave a young—or old—disciple exposed to solitude, danger, and death?

Beautiful Rebbe Barukh—he left the serenity of his palace and the comfort of his faith to save a young man by helping him surmount his fear and cope with his doubts . . . Admirable Rebbe Barukh, who, in order to assist his disciple, chose to open and close the same gates he did, confront the same perils he did, approach the same abyss he did . . . and be bruised by the same dark flames that bruised him.

He risked not only his life for someone else's, but also his faith for someone else's: that was his concept—and the Besht's too—of *Ahavat-Israel.* He was angry? Naturally he was. He was angry because he cared, because he was concerned, because he was present to anyone in need of human presence.

What did he tell the young student?

I know there are questions that have no answers; there is a suffering that has no name; there is injustice in God's creation—and there are reasons enough for man to explode with rage. I know there are reasons for you to be angry. Good. Let us be angry. Together.

# The Holy Seer
# of Lublin

This is one of the most enigmatic episodes in Hasidic literature—an episode that chroniclers and storytellers are still reluctant to explain, or even explore.

The year: 1814.

The place: Lublin. Inside the House of Study, Hasidim—old and young, learned and unlearned, innkeepers and travelers—participate in the traditional ceremony of rejoicing with the Torah.

They have come in the hundreds, and more, from beyond mountains and rivers; they have crossed many borders and overcome many obstacles to be here tonight.

The Beit Midrash has never known such crowds or such fervor. With their old Master, the holy Seer of Lublin in their midst, the weak forget their weakness, the old are unaware of their age. Tonight, the poor are less poor, the sick forget their illnesses. Tonight, all worries are forbidden.

Surrounding their Master, people sing and dance with frenzy. Like him, with him, they lift the

Holy Scrolls higher and higher, as if to follow them—and follow *him*—and they do. He carries them away, far away. They trust him. What if they do not know the outcome or the purpose of his secret plan: *he* does, and that should be enough, and it is. What matters is to be present. Hasn't he taught them that passion succeeds where reason fails? Tonight they are consumed by passion.

They all feel it now: this celebration is unlike any other. Every word reverberates in higher spheres, every impulse is echoed in invisible palaces up there, in heaven, where Israel's fate is being determined—and mankind's too.

Just before the holiday the Seer had dispatched emissaries to friends and disciples, urging them to mark this Simhat Torah with particular emphasis. "I have one favor to ask of you," he told his old friend Reb Israel, the Maggid of Kozhenitz. "Rejoice on this festive event, let yourself go, let your soul soar."

And to his own community, gathered from all over his kingdom, he repeated over and over again: "Drink and celebrate—it's an order. And if your ecstasy is pure enough, contagious enough, it will last forever—I promise you that."

In spite of his age and his fatigue, he himself leads the assembly with astonishing vigor. It's as though his intention is to move the entire creation from darkness to redemption.

Yes, now it's clear to everyone: this holiday is

destined to be special; man's future hinges upon it. Let Israel attain perfection through joy—and man will know no more anguish.

"*Sissou vesimkhou besimkhat Torah*," orders the Master. And the Hasidim obey. They let go of their senses until they see nothing and nobody. And they fail to notice when the Master suddenly breaks away from the crowd and moves slowly, quietly, toward the door. Still unnoticed, he opens it, and retires into his private study. He stays there all alone, while down below, on *his* orders, the happy, exuberant Hasidim continue to celebrate.

No one knows what he did there—no one knows what really happened to him then. All we know is that at one point the Rebbetzin heard strange noises coming from the Seer's study: sounds like those of a child weeping. She rushed into the room and shrieked with fear. The room was empty.

Down below, they heard the scream. And for a second they remained frozen in silence. Then they heard the Rebbetzin crying: "He told me to keep an eye on him—now he is gone, gone. He has been taken away."

Taken away? By whom? Why? Where? The Rebbetzin didn't know. She claimed to have seen monstrously big hands pulling the Rebbe out the window—that was all.

Those who were there will never forget that night. Everyone ran into the street. The night was dark, opaque. Minutes went by. Nothing. The Rebbe? Swallowed by darkness.

Hours went by. Still nothing.

Suddenly, fifty feet away from the House of Study, a certain Reb Eliezer of Khmelnik perceived a weak moaning in the shadows. Approaching, he saw a man lying on the ground, twisting with pain. "Who are you?" asked Reb Eliezer.

"Yaakov-Yitzhak, son of Meitil," whispered the man.

Reb Eliezer called out for help. The older Hasidim quickly conferred on who should carry their stricken Master—and how. Reb Shmuel of Karov held his head and heard him softly intone ancient poignant lamentations, repeating the words: "And the abyss calls for another abyss."

Thus ended, prematurely, tragically, a memorable celebration which was meant to last beyond the night. Having put their Master to bed, the Hasidim, silent and heartbroken, returned to the House of Study. Defeated.

What had happened? Who had done what to the old Seer of Lublin? And what had *he* done . . . to whom? To himself? No one knows—no one will ever know.

Hasidic literature has shrouded this disturbing episode in secrecy. It is almost considered taboo. A strange conspiracy of silence has surrounded it ever since it took place.

Some sources refer to it cryptically as the Great

Fall—*hanefila hagdola*—without entering into details. Usually they add the expression *kayadoua*—"as everybody knows." And, as usual, it means the opposite. Whenever Hasidic texts say *kayadoua*, it means that nobody knows. Or that nobody is supposed to know.

Most sources indicate that the Great Fall had important metaphysical or mystical implications. Why the Fall? Had the old Master *fallen* from his second-floor window? The window, according to testimony, was too narrow for a man his size to pass through. And also, empty bottles were left standing intact on the sill.

So the feeling persisted that the accident had some connection with the supernatural. It must have been the work—or the vengeance—of Satan, who surely resented the holy Seer's messianic experiments, which no one may conduct with impunity.

Lately, the Rebbe of Lublin had been involved in perilous activities, trying to use Napoleon's wars to precipitate events—and he was punished. That was the general belief. Seeking and failing to achieve cosmic salvation, the Rebbe's quest had ended in personal catastrophe. The fact is that he never recovered. He stayed in bed for forty-four weeks. When he died, the entire Hasidic world went into mourning.

For he was one of its most dazzling and most secretive figures. His impact was felt throughout its communities from Galicia to the Ukraine. Some of the greatest Masters had been his disciples. How many? Some say sixty. Others, one hundred twenty; and still others, four hundred. What's the difference? Hasidism is better known for its touching fantasy than for its accuracy. All agree that Lublin was one of the most dynamic centers of the Hasidic movement.

Said Rebbe Naphtali of Ropshitz: "The holy Seer is dead—and the world goes on? I don't understand."

Said Rebbe Moshe of Ujhely: "Our Master possessed all the qualities and virtues of the Prophet Isaiah—except that he did not dwell in the Holy Land."

Ouri, the Seraphin of Strelisk, remarked: "Lublin *was* the Holy Land: our Master's court was Jerusalem; his House of Study, the Temple; his private study, the sanctuary; and in his voice, the heavenly voice could be heard."

And Rebbe Tzvi-Hersh of Ziditchoiv said: "As long as our holy Master was alive, we would gather around him, and place our arms on each other's shoulders, and thus were able to reach heaven. Now, with him gone, we have no longer the strength to look up. Even our dreams have changed."


In order to understand Lublin and its messianic currents and undercurrents, we must look at the general setting. Before we investigate the accident, we must get acquainted with the victim—and his times.

We are at the beginning of the nineteenth century. Nations wage wars and man is their eternal victim. Europe is upside down, churning in blood and fury. The era of Enlightenment has brought forth its own myths, its own prisons, its own darkness. Wars, wars, more wars. Frontiers, systems, loyalties come and go. The earth trembles. Priests change their style, kings lose their thrones, and sometimes even their heads, paving the way for other kings, other kinds of kings. Ultimately, judges and victims change places; only the executioner remains the same.

Emperor Napoleon has reached the Holy Land, invaded Russia and dreams of world domination. Military conquest does not satisfy him; wherever his armies appear, they bring emancipation. But is it good for Jews? Or not?

In Eastern Europe, opinions are divided. Persecuted by hereditary fanatic Russian and Polish Jew-haters, the Jews feel just as threatened by Austrian liberals. They must opt for either spiritual or physical safety—the two seem to be incompatible.

Rebbe Shneur-Zalmen of Ladi, the eminent Hasidic thinker and teacher, says: "I prefer Czar Alexander; under his rule, we suffer—but we remain united and unblemished as Jews. Under Napoleon, it will be the opposite."

Reb Mendel of Riminov, on the other hand, favors Napoleon, in whom he sees the incarnation of the legendary Gog of Magog, who will be defeated by the Messiah. But in order to become Gog of Magog, he must first be victorious. So some opponents and skeptics say that Napoleon's *second* military headquarters, headed by Reb Mendel, are in Riminov.

In the Hasidic universe, everyone's mind is set on the messianic dimension of the apocalyptic events. All these defeats and victories succeeding one another. All this blood being shed on all sides. Clearly, the end of the world is near. So why not take the initiative and hasten it? It could save Jewish lives; in fact, nothing else could save them. The Jews need the Messiah as never before. Since he is so near, why wait for him? Why not run *to* him?

Moreover, the times seemed ripe. The wars. The total upheavals. The *Chevlei Mashiah:* the pangs of messianic birth. All the symptoms, all the signs were there. That is why the three conspirators—Reb Mendel of Riminov, the Maggid of Kozhenitz, and the Seer of Lublin—worked on their plan so feverishly. They met secretly to compare notes and coordinate their activities. Often the Seer disappeared from Lublin, and no one would know where he had gone. In fact, he regularly went to Kozhenitz or to Riminov—for strategy sessions. They really believed that with their *kavanot* and *yikhudim,* with their words and deeds, they could influence events and developments on the battlefield.

Said Reb Mendel of Riminov: "Let the blood flow from Pristik to Riminov—as long as it means that redemption is imminent."

One *Kol Nidre* evening, the Maggid of Kozhenitz opened the Holy Ark and exclaimed: *"Ribono shel olam*, Master of the Universe, please say *salakhti kidvarekha*—say that you have forgiven our sins. And send us the redeemer. If you need a Tzaddik, Reb Mendel of Riminov is one. If you need a Prophet, the Seer of Lublin is one. If you need a penitent, I, Israel, son of Sarah of Kozhenitz, proclaim here and now that I am ready for sacrifice in the name of the living community of Israel."

What, then, went wrong? Why hasn't the Messiah come? The three Masters, and their friends and allies, could not agree on tactics. That's why. Had they all supported Napoleon, he would have been Gog of Magog. And would have conquered the world, only to lose it to the Messiah. The trouble was that except for Reb Mendel of Riminov, no one gave the French Emperor unqualified support. Legend has it that Napoleon knew this and came clandestinely to plead with the Maggid of Kozhenitz . . . to win him over completely. He failed—and lost the war.

Another legend claims that one of the Seer's sons served in the Austrian army. Somehow—who knows how?—he was introduced to Napoleon at a military parade. And the Emperor told him: "Tell your father that I am not afraid of him." Clearly, he had to lose.

After Waterloo, following the Seer's plea, the three conspirators decided to make one last attempt on Simhat Torah. Again, had they rejoiced on that holiday, as only they could rejoice, the event might have occurred. But —*lo ikhshar dara*—the generation wasn't ready. The Maggid of Kozhenitz died a week before Simhat Torah, on the eve of Succoth, and the Seer had his famous Great Fall.

The accident caused great joy among his opponents, the Mitnagdim. But the Seer remarked: "They are silly to overdo it. I can assure them that when I die, they will not be able to drink to the occasion—not even a glass of water." Sure enough, he died on the ninth day of Av, which is a day of mourning and fasting. Even for Mitnagdim.


Who *was* the Seer?

From personal testimonies and recollections of disciples and followers, we possess enough material to piece together his biography and his portrait.

We know that Rebbe Yaakov-Yitzhak Horowitz was born in 1745 in a village near Tarnigrod in Poland. He grew up in the home of his grandfather, Reb Kopel, in Yusepov.

Three times married, he was the father of four sons and a daughter—and the author of three important books of commentaries.

Having had a solitary childhood, he was attracted to the young and vibrant Hasidic movement, first as disciple and then as Master. He settled in Lublin around 1800. Active in Jewish politics of the times, he unsuccessfully fought for the emancipation of the Jews, but successfully fought their induction into military service.

A founder of a school, he established no dynasty of his own. His *disciples* became leaders in their own right.

People flocked to him from near and far, even from nonreligious circles. The renowned Professor Bernard was his personal physician and friend.

Tall, robust, tense, extremely perceptive, and eloquent, he was unquestionably charismatic; he seemed always to be the center of his surroundings. His entire being radiated wisdom, beauty, and authority. He rarely said "I"—rather, he said "We." He rarely ate in public. There was something regal about his personality.

In his presence, one felt shaken, purified . . . transformed. What struck people most were his eyes—one bigger than the other—which often took on a disquieting fixity when looking at someone. Hasidim were convinced that he was searching their inner depths. Nothing resisted his gaze, neither time nor space. He would go to the window and observe what was happening continents away, centuries before. It is said of him that he was able to trace one's soul back to Cain or Abel, and determine precisely how many times it had migrated since—and where.

His surname—the Seer—has remained his, exclusively. Other Masters were endowed with powers, but none with his vision. In his early youth he prayed to God to take it away; he found it a burden, and depressing. He saw too much, too far. But his plea was not answered.

Some legends maintain that during three—or seven—years he chose not to lift his eyes from the ground, so as not to see the world. Others claim that for seven years he chose silence, so as not to use and abuse language.

Though he was accessible, generous, and compassionate, there existed between him and his followers a kind of barrier which prevented them from coming too close, from lifting the veil.

Serious, at times melancholy, he would sit with his close disciples once a week and try to create a cheerful atmosphere. That was on Saturday nights, at the meal called *melave-malka*, during which Hasidim accompany the Queen Shabbat on her way to exile for another week. At that meal the Master would encourage his followers to speak up and entertain the audience.

During weekdays he was often withdrawn, and even forbidding. Listen to an anecdote: A Hasid who had just been received by the holy Seer was so enraptured that he told a friend of his: "You know? The Rebbe of Lublin looks . . . looks like an angry lion."—"Have you ever seen an angry lion?" asked the friend.—"As a matter of fact, no."—No? Then

how do you know what an angry lion looks like?—
"Well—I didn't know. *Now* I do," said the Hasid.

At the age of three, Yaakov-Yitzhak often ran
away from *heder*—for which he was punished by his
teacher, until the *melamed* followed him into the
forest—surreptitiously, of course—and heard him
shout *Sh'ma Israel:* Listen, Israel—God is our God.
Only then did his teacher stop punishing him.

But his father wanted to know: "Why are you
wasting your time in the forest? Why do you go
there?"—"I am looking for God," said the three-
year-old boy.—"Isn't God everywhere?" asked the
father. "And isn't He everywhere the same?"—"He
is—but I am not," replied the child.

At fourteen he went to Yeshiva. First at Zhul-
kova, where he studied under the renowned Talmudist Reb Moshe-Hersh Meisels, and then under
the celebrated Reb Shmelke of Nikolsburg, in
Shineve. There the regime was extremely rigorous.
An average day meant fourteen hours for study,
four hours for prayer, four for sleep, one hour for
communal activity, a half hour for meals and another half hour for rest. Only the young Yaakov-
Yitzhak was exempt from these rules.

For a while he led a marginal existence. Legend
has it that he concealed his erudition. Only Reb
Shmelke knew his true value, and permitted him to
go his own way. To fast, to seek solitude. To purify

his mind and soul through *dvekut*—concentration, attachment—and prayer. When Yaakov-Yitzhak prays, remarked Reb Shmelke, the heavenly host of angels say Amen.

It was there, in Shineve, that he decided to close his eyes to the visible world and live the life of the blind: no solitude equals theirs. But later he had to open his eyes, for his solitude was threatened: he was getting married. And once again we stumble on a dramatic incident.

The marriage was arranged by Reb Shmelke and Yaakov-Yitzhak's grandfather, Reb Kopel. The girl? From a good family, naturally. Her father was a wealthy merchant, with dealings near Krasnobrad. The groom, when informed of the decision, agreed. How could he say no to his teacher and to his beloved grandfather? A date was set. Preparations began amid the usual excitement.

Many people came to attend the ceremony. Let us look in on them as they partake of the customary "groom's meal" on the eve of the wedding. They sing, they play music, they laugh. The groom delivers a speech. At one point he turns to his grandfather with a peculiar request: he would like to see the bride. General amazement. What? Now? Before the ceremony? Doesn't he trust his grandfather? But Yaakov-Yitzhak, nicknamed Reb Itzikl, quotes the Talmud: A man ought not to take a woman as his wife unless he has seen her first. Well, since the Talmud is on his side, the grandfather has no choice but to satisfy his whim. The bride is fetched from her chambers to meet her fiancé. Reb Itzikl lifts the veil—and begins to shiver. The bride leaves, and he is still shivering.

It's all right, people think; he has never seen a woman before, let alone his own. Only natural that he reacts this way.

When the meal is over and the guests have left, the groom turns to his parents and declares flatly: "I am not going to marry her. Let us go away, far away, far from here—far from her. We are not suited for each other."

You can imagine their reaction. "What happened, Itzikl? All the time you said yes, now all of a sudden you say no. What has come over you?"

"Nothing," says the groom. "Only that I have seen her. That's enough. I don't like her; she is not for me."

"How do you know?"

And Itzikl replies: "I have seen her face, the face of a stranger."

They implore him, they plead with him: to offend and shame a nice Jewish girl publicly is a sin, an outrage. Reb Itzikl is obstinate. Finally his father has an idea: marry her—and divorce her. And that is what he did. He married her and left as soon as the ceremony was over. He didn't even bother to wait until the next day. Or to change clothes. He ran away. Where? Two versions: to Mezeritch or to Lizensk. From there he sent her a divorce.

To justify his behavior, Hasidic legend tells us that he was lucky to have run away: she was not right for him. The proof? *Kayadoua*—as everybody knows—she later left her family and her people and married a Polish nobleman. And that was what he had seen at their first meeting.

The escape itself inspired many a Hasidic storyteller. Several versions offer variations on the same theme. He ran away without knowing where he was going. He was tired, hungry, and cold. He was picked up by coachmen who were on their way to Lizensk or Mezeritch. Somehow, during a stopover at an inn, a beautiful woman tried to seduce him. He ran away—which made Rebbe Elimelekh call him Joseph Hatzaddik, the Just, after the biblical Joseph.

A legend: On his way to Mezeritch—not Lizensk—Reb Itzikl lost his way as he crossed an immense, thick forest. Strong winds began to blow. A snowstorm began to rage. Frozen, tired, blind with fatigue and fear, Reb Itzikl felt close to death. He leaned against a tree and recited the *Vidui*, the last confession before death.

He stopped in the middle, for suddenly the storm subsided and so did the wind. The forest became hospitable. There seemed to be a way out and Reb Itzikl began to walk. Eventually he saw a light. A house. No, a castle. A palace. Good, he will knock at the door, enter and rest, and be warm. He did just that. The castle seemed empty, though it wasn't, after all. A woman lived there. Alone. A beautiful woman—the most beautiful woman alive. She invited him to come and sit next to her; her voice was soft and caressing—never before had he heard anything like it.

"I am unattached and alone," she whispered. "Come closer; I have been waiting for you, for you alone."

Reb Itzikl felt tempted, but only for a fleeting second. For he immediately remembered: It is forbidden. What will God get from my pleasure? God, too, was waiting. And so he ran from the castle, away from the woman, away from temptation. And then he realized that it had all been an illusion. There was no castle, no woman—only the forest.

When he arrived in Mezeritch, the great Maggid received him with unusual affection: "The other side—the evil impulse—tried to get you. I am glad you won."

Reb Itzikl stayed there a while. He lived in poverty; he couldn't even afford challah for Shabbat. But to be close to the undisputed leader of the movement was his reward. He learned the principles of the Baal Shem Tov's new way of life, based on love of man and love of God. He was in a constant state of exultation. Ancient words came to life;

human encounters offered new meaning. He observed the singular relations between Master and followers, as they existed in Mezeritch: the disciple *chose* his Rebbe, to whom he then owed absolute allegiance. He also learned the vital importance of friendship in Hasidism. And of beauty. And sincerity. Mezeritch was a laboratory: those who came as disciples left as teachers.

The Maggid loved Reb Itzikl. Of him he said: "A soul like his has not been sent to us since the times of the Prophets."

But like most of his friends who gathered in Mezeritch, the Seer didn't stay there permanently. In due time he moved to Lizensk, where he became the protégé of Rebbe Elimelekh. There, too, he began by leading an isolated life—away from people, avoiding fellow students, bent on silence and truth. And there an incident occurred which one must remember when exploring the mystery of his Great Fall.

One day Reb Itzikl left Rebbe Elimelekh's House of Study and went for a walk in the woods. He climbed a hill, then a mountain, and sat down on a rock projecting over an abyss. There he meditated on the meaning of life and the futility of man's endeavors. God is God and man is small—so small; Reb Itzikl felt grateful to God for noticing man at all. I wish I could give Him something, he thought. But I have nothing, I possess nothing. All I can ever offer Him is myself. So he stood up, ready to throw himself over the precipice. Fortunately, it so happened that a certain Reb Salke was standing not too far behind him. He caught him in time, and brought him back to Lizensk. Years later the Seer would often remind Reb Salke of the incident, and add cryptically: "Yes, Salke, we remember what you have done for us in Lizensk—that is why our love for you is not whole."

How many years did he stay in Lizensk? This is not clear. He stayed long enough to become Reb Elimelekh's favorite disciple. He would be asked to take care of young, scholarly followers. To teach them, guide them—open them to Hasidic fervor. Thus the disciple became the Rebbe. And began attracting followers of his own. Whereupon the old Rebbe Elimelekh felt hurt and betrayed. He asked Reb Itzikl to wait before establishing his own community. Too late. The *first* break in the life of the young movement could not be avoided. The Seer moved to Lanzhut, then to Rozvadov and finally to Lublin—the new center, the youngest, the most dynamic in Hasidism.

As had happened in Mezeritch and Lizensk, an attempt was made in Lublin to intensify Jewish life—to reconstruct the Jewish world. Through simple prayers, simple stories. And human contact. People mattered more than doctrines.

Here the Seer's followers lived together, sharing possessions as well as dreams. They came here the way their forefathers had gathered in Jerusalem long ago: to be together, to participate in new experiences. Here, one could forget one's misery, one's hunger; one's earthly problems mattered less or not at all. Close to the holy Seer, one found meaning in what seemed to have none. In Lublin, one was again allowed to see Jewishness as a magnificent adventure.

In Lublin we learned that God is present everywhere and man can talk to Him about all his problems—and not only about theology. And we also learned that the Rebbe must be available to every one of his followers and listen to their pleas on any level, and be their ally on any terms.

What is Hasidism if not an attempt to tear down everything that separates one man from another—and from himself? Hasidism is against the walls that exist between God and man, creation and creature, thought and deed, past and present, reality and soul: the secret lies in oneness.

In Lublin the Hasid could dream again—without guilt feelings—of his own possibilities. To the lonely Jew, the Seer said: "God, too, is alone—alone because of you." To the melancholy Jew, he said: "God too is sad—sad because of you." To the poverty-stricken Jew, he said: "It is up to you to alter your condition. You can defeat misfortune; invoke joy or create it, and things will change for you and others as well." For this is basic to the Hasidic message: there is total interdependence between man and heaven; both have an effect on one another.

Like other Masters, the Seer advocated passion and compassion, and enthusiasm, fervor—*hitlahavut*—fervor, above all. "I prefer an opponent—a passionate Mitnagged—rather than a lukewarm Hasid," he said. For absence of fire, absence of passion, leads to indifference and resignation—in other words, to death. What is worse than suffering? Indifference. What is worse than despair? Resignation—the inability to be moved, to let oneself go, to let one's imagination catch fire.

At that moment in Eastern Europe, when hundreds of Jewish communities felt abandoned by mankind and noticed by the enemy alone, this was a powerful, irresistible message.

Thus, by putting the emphasis on *Ahavat Israel*, on its repercussions in higher spheres, on its redemptive quality, Hasidism kept alive many Jews who came close to giving in to shame and remorse and hopelessness. And it restored to the Jew the idea of joy.

This is why in less than fifty years the Beshtian movement swept through Eastern Europe's Jewish communities. The spark kindled between Kossov and Kitev now illuminated them all.

Which was good—and not so good. There were many Hasidim, and that was good. But there were

many Tzaddikim, and that was less good. Soon they
would begin quarreling and the movement would
lose something of its original purity.

From Mezeritch and Lizensk came numerous
Tzaddikim. They were active in the Ukraine, in
White Russia, in Lithuania, in Hungary, and, naturally, in Galicia. Suddenly it was so easy to be a
Jew—a Hasidic Jew: all you had to do was to choose
a Rebbe for yourself. He knew all the answers; his
was the supreme authority.

The Seer, conscious of the perils inherent in
success, referred to them occasionally: "I prefer a
rascal who knows that he is a rascal to a Tzaddik
who knows that he is a Tzaddik." He also said:
"Tzaddikim are sinners too, except that they don't
know it. In the other world, they are led into hell—
and they believe they're on a visit, or on a mission to
help those who are there permanently, but then the
gates are shut and they stay inside." And repeating
the last sentence, the Seer would laugh and say:
"Oh yes, they stay inside."

Except for Reb Barukh of Medzebozh, the
Besht's grandson, the Seer maintained cordial and
even friendly relations with most of his illustrious
contemporaries. He would visit them and they
would visit him. His quarrel with Reb Barukh? At
the Shabbat meal the Seer would sit with his followers, while Reb Barukh would have his wife and
daughters at the table. And yet, lest you accuse the

Seer of anti-feminism, mention should be made of his rather liberal attitude on women's rights. Unlike many Rebbes, he permitted them to dress elegantly. Also, he received them, and occasionally he even accompanied them to the door.

Gentiles were attracted to him as well. One of them, the famous Count Csartorinsky, was received with special warmth in Lublin. A Hasid wondered aloud: "Why him and not me? I, at least, am a little bit of a Jew, while the Count is not?"—Answered the Seer: "I prefer a Gentile who is Gentile to a Jew who is only partly, or half-heartedly, Jewish."

Like the Besht, he knew and loved nature— and brought it back into Jewish life. Everything in creation testifies for God's work, he said. All things are examples. Take a raven, for instance. He has three distinguishing marks. One: he accepts no strangers in his circle; if he shouts so loud, it is so as not to hear outsiders. Two: he is convinced that in the world of birds he alone exists—that other birds are nothing but ravens in disguise. Three: a raven does not tolerate loneliness; the moment he loses his way and breaks away from his companions, he faces dark anguish and death.

In the spirit of Hasidism, the Seer urged his followers to encourage belief in two cardinal principles: *emunat-Tzaddikim* and *dibuk-haverim*—faith in the master and fidelity to friends.

And he did love his followers, both collectively and individually. He would call each and every one of them Yidele—the diminutive for Yid, the Jew. He listened to their sorrows and shared in their pain. More than in Mezeritch, more even than in Lizensk, the Rebbe was an integral part of the individual Hasid's life.

Teacher, guide, friend—the Seer was also miracle-maker. In Lublin, miracles occupied the forefront. People came for miracles, and found them. Innumerable legends speak of the Seer's powers. It was enough for the poor, desperate men and women to implore him to intercede on their behalf, and heaven would submit to his will. Lublin was the people's last recourse. When everything else failed, they went to the Rebbe. Financial disasters. Health problems. Doubts, crises, threats. The Seer had cures for every ailment.

I know all this may seem shocking, even revolting to the rationalists among us. But one must look at the situation in its entirety. Before judging, one must take into consideration the immense suffering that Jews were subjected to. Caught in ever-growing despair, what they needed most was a reason to believe. The very possibility of believing was a miracle in itself. That was why Tzaddikim performed miracles. To strike the imagination. To inspire awe. To help souls open themselves to faith and hope. *Vayar Israel et hayad hagdola asher assa adoshem bemitzrayim*—and the Jews saw the miracles in Egypt; thanks to them, they could believe. What does the Tzaddik do? asked the Seer of Lublin.

Through his prayer he reveals God's grandeur. The miracle? Meant to propagate man's faith in God— that whenever man speaks, God listens; and that the laws of the soul are more important than those of nature.

Did the Seer have *ruakh-hakodesh?* Was he endowed with prophetic powers? His followers were convinced of it, and he himself never denied it. Indeed, he made a point of occasionally issuing legal decisions based on his clairvoyance. An example: A woman was accused of adultery. Said he: "Did anyone see her commit the sin?"—"No, but she was seen as she entered a room alone with a man."—"Is that all?" said the Rebbe. "Then I tell you she is innocent." And he explained: "I know that in your hearts there is a doubt; still, to protect a person, I am entitled to invoke my inner sight against your doubts."

Such was the nature of all his miracles. He used them *for* the community of Israel; they were but *means* to an end, namely, to comfort and console, to encourage and uplift those lonely human beings who felt unworthy of God's attention.

He himself, incidentally, would sometimes voice remarks that led observers to assume that he did not take his miracle-making too seriously. That people believed in them was all right, but he was too intelligent, too lucid not to laugh at himself; he had an exquisite sense of humor.

A story: Rebbe Levi-Yitzhak of Berditchev, his

older friend and companion, admonished him one day for making a public display of his mystical powers: "Is this what I taught you?" he asked. — "I am sorry you feel that way," said the Seer. "Just give me the order and I shall stop immediately." — "No, no," said the Berditchever, "you may continue, you may."

One of his younger sons, who was present at the meeting, asked him later: "Did you really mean it, Father? Were you ready to give up your *ruakh-hakodesh*, your prophetic gift?" — "Oh no," said the Seer, laughing. "Thanks to my second sight, I knew in advance that he would *not* ask me to stop."

"I dislike fools," he said. "Should I see, in the world of truth, a fool being led into paradise and given all the honors, I would run from street to street and shout: 'Fools remain fools; I don't envy you.' "

He also said: "People go to Riminov to get sustenance and to Kozhenitz to get cures. But they come to Lublin to get the Hasidic fire."

To a Hasid who complained that he suffered from impure, alien thoughts, he said: "Alien? They are not alien—they are *yours.*"

A Hasid came to ask for permission to spend Shabbat with the Maggid of Kozhenitz. "What kind of Hasid are you?" said the Seer. "When I was a

Hasid, I went to see all the Masters—did I ask anyone's permission?"

A great scholar—and opponent of Hasidism—in Lublin, Reb Azriel Hurwitz, nicknamed *"Der Eizerner Kop,"* once had a friendly conversation with the Seer. "I don't understand," said he. "I am more erudite than you, more learned and a better scholar than you, and yet people come to you and not to me. Why is that?"

"I don't know," answered the holy Seer. "Perhaps we ought to turn the question into an answer. You don't understand why people don't come to you, that's why they don't come. I don't understand why they *do* come, that's why they come."

Another time, the same Reb Azriel said to him: "Reb Itzikl, people call you Tzaddik, whereas both you and I know that you are not. Why not admit it publicly? If you do, they will go away." — "Perfect," said the Seer. "Good idea."

The following Shabbat, before the reading of the Torah, he ascended the bimah and declared: "I want you all to know that I am not a Tzaddik; on the contrary, I am a sinner. I do not study enough, nor do I pray enough. I do not serve God the way I should. So—go and find yourself another Rebbe, worthier of your trust."

Naturally, the reaction was unanimous: Our

Master is even greater than we thought. He is the greatest of all—look at his humility.

Next, Reb Azriel suggested that the Seer do the opposite: that he state publicly that he was a true Tzaddik, so the people would resent his vanity and leave him alone. But the Seer refused, saying: "I agree with you that I am *not* a Tzaddik—but I am not a liar either."

In spite of their friendly arguments and Reb Azriel's open, relentless hostility to Hasidism and Hasidim, the Seer deeply respected his scholarship; he would even send the best of his disciples to study under him.

What he himself had to give was not learning, though he was learned, but the art of human relations, which, of course, goes beyond human relations. He taught his followers not how to study but how to listen, how to share, how to feel, how to pray, how to laugh, how to hope—how to live. What the Besht had done for his followers, the Seer did for his: he gave them a sense of dignity. Simple innkeepers, city coachmen, forsaken villagers came to Lublin once a year, and that was enough to make them feel Jewish, human—and part of the Jewish people. What Kant said of himself—that because of his books, people would no longer think as before—was, in a larger sense, true of the Seer. Once he entered the lives of his followers, they no longer lived as before. It is said that even his opponents fell under his spell: those who attended his "third meals" of Shabbat would sit down as opponents and get up as admirers.

And yet, he who gave so much to others was himself longing for change. He gave joy to others but rarely to himself. Often he would remark: "Strange—people come to me sad and leave happy; whereas I . . . I stay with my sadness; mine is a black fire." In moments of doubt he would groan: "Woe to the generation whose leader I am."

He sought joy with such intensity that he ignored other considerations. Said he: "I prefer a simple Jew who prays with joy to a sage who studies with sadness."

A notorious sinner in Lublin had free access to him, for the Rebbe enjoyed his company. To his Hasidim who cautiously voiced surprise, he explained: "I like him because he is cheerful. When *you* commit a sin you immediately regret it; you repent for the pleasure you have felt. Not he. His joy continues."

Once he asked: "Do you know the real sin of our forefathers in the desert? Not their rebellious behavior, but their ensuing depression."

To fight depression, he had—like Reb Barukh—a kind of clown, a troubadour, a house comic—Reb Mordechai Rakover—who would tell him jokes to make him laugh.

With the exception of Rebbe Nahman of Bratzlav, no other Hasidic Master placed such emphasis on the concept of exuberance and celebration in his teachings. In Lublin, Hasidim were urged to live not only in fear of God but also in fear for God and, above all, in joy with God.

Legend has it that Reb Mendel Riminover, who wanted his followers to aspire to silence through quiet meditation, was shocked when he discovered the cheerful mood of Lublin. He looked at the Hasidim at services and uttered a simple *"Na"*—and all were struck with awe and fear. Whereupon the Seer uttered a simple *"Ho"*—and they happily resumed their singing and hand clapping.

Exuberance, joy, celebration, enthusiasm, fervor, ecstasy: this is what the Seer, in Lublin, gave his disciples and followers—as weapons to fight melancholy, sadness, and despair.

For he, too, seems to have been haunted by sadness. Why? Because of his tragic break with his teacher, Rebbe Elimelekh? No, he was melancholic before their first meeting. Because of his opponents *outside* the movement? The early Maskilim who preached emancipation? Or the militant Mitnagdim, who once, just before Rosh Hashana, drove him out of Lublin? Well—other Masters had similar troubles and worse experiences.

But then they, too, seem to have been subject to similar spells of depression. From the Besht to the Maggid, to Reb Levi-Yitzhak, to Reb Barukh, to Reb Elimelekh, to the Kotzker—all endured pain and anguish. The reasons were manifold. Mystically inclined, they constantly thought of the Shekhina suffering in exile, and if the Shekhina suffered, how could *they* not suffer with her? The Seer of Lublin said: "A Hasid, like a child, should cry and laugh at the same time." And he explained how he managed to combine the two when lamenting over the Shekhina's suffering every night at midnight: "Imagine an exiled king who visits his friend; the friend is sad that the king is in exile, but still he is happy to be seeing him."

There were other reasons for their melancholy. Most Hasidim came to the Rebbe to unburden themselves of their misery and anxieties. And the Rebbe listened—listened well. And empathized. And identified. The Hasid knew that the Rebbe alone understood him, so the Rebbe had to justify his trust. Well, how long can one go on hearing tales of woe and tears? Of hungry children and persecuted fathers? Week after week, day after day, hour after hour the Rebbe would listen to the misfortunes of his people in the various small communities ruled mostly by wicked landowners. How could he stay immune? One morning he had to wake up with a broken heart.

But in the case of the Seer of Lublin, there were other elements, of a more personal nature, that weighed on his mood.

He survived both his Master, Rebbe Elimelekh, and his successor, the "Jew of Pshiskhe." He had hurt the former and was hurt by the latter.

In truth, one fails to understand. Why had he been in such a hurry? Why hadn't he heeded Rebbe Elimelekh's pathetic pleas to wait and inherit his kingdom . . . later? Why had he inflicted such suffering on the old teacher? And why did he complain when the same thing happened to him? What the Seer had done to his Master, the Jew of Pshiskhe did to *his*. The Seer, too, felt rejected, betrayed. Rebbe Elimelekh had forseen it. He had warned the Seer: You have no pity for my old age—or for yours.

The break between Lublin and Pshiskhe was tragic for both leaders. There were no major differences between Lizensk and Lublin, but there were between Lublin and Pshiskhe. The young rebels claimed that Hasidism in Lublin had become too popular, too popularized; they rejected its emphasis on miracles and advocated instead a return to study, devotion, self-fulfillment—a return to the true source of their inspiration. Relations between them grew bitter, angry. Intrigues, gossip, clannishness turned brother against brother, father against son. Several times the Jew of Pshiskhe came personally to plead with his Master not to reject him, not to condemn him. The wounds eventually healed, but the scars remained.

Before the Jew of Pshiskhe passed away, he said: "I had the choice; it was to be either he or I. Since my prayers could save only one life, I preferred it to be his."

When the Seer learned of his death, he wept

and said: "He will be our emissary in heaven to hasten the coming of the Messiah." His disciples wept too, so much so that he had to console them: "True," he said, "a great teacher died—but remember: God is alive; don't cry."

His was the tragedy of the survivor. He felt alone. Rejected by both his Master and his favorite disciple. He still had friends, followers, companions, particularly the Maggid of Kozhenitz and Reb Mendel or Riminov, his two co-conspirators. Together, the three Rebbes attempted to shake the laws of time and bring redemption. The story of that mystical conspiracy is among the most touching and moving projects in Hasidic or messianic literature. It ended in failure. All three died in the same year. And the Seer—who had seen so far and so deep—must have guessed from the beginning that the Messiah would not come, not yet, not before a long time. How could he help being sad?

On his deathbed, he wanted his third wife to promise him not to remarry. She refused. He did not insist. He remained quiet, at peace. Then he began reciting *Sh'ma Israel* with increasing passion, his face aflame as never before.

In conclusion, what did happen on that Simhat Torah evening in Lublin? What caused the accident? Was it an accident? What kind of an accident?

Why did the Seer leave the exuberant festivities? Why did he stop dancing? Why did he tell the Rebbetzin to keep an eye on him? Was he afraid? And if so—of what, of whom?

Was it a sudden attack of sadness, of depression? Was it his way of telling God: Either You save Your people—or erase me from Your book? I no longer wish to go on living—unless You put an end to Jewish suffering?

Could it be that, having failed to bring the Messiah through joy, he thought of trying . . . despair?

Perhaps he realized suddenly that it was too early for real redemption. That the ruins of Jerusalem would not disappear so soon. His old Master was gone. His young disciple and successor was gone. His trusted companion, the Maggid of Kozhenitz, was gone. His allies and accomplices were disarmed. He must have felt lonelier than ever—more heartbroken than ever.

Perhaps he remembered the first time, in his youth, in Lizensk, when he had felt the irresistible urge to jump into the abyss and become an offering to God. To God—who had refused his gift of joy.

Could it also be that in a sudden flash of fear the Seer had a glimpse of the distant future when night would descend upon the Jewish people and particularly upon its most compassionate and generous children—those of the Hasidic community? Was that why he strayed outside? To wait under the somber sky, abandoned and shattered, to wait and wait through several generations, if necessary, for other victims of other catastrophes?

Lublin: the sanctuary, the center for messianic dreamers. Lublin then, Lublin now.

Somewhere a group of Hasidim joins a nocturnal procession. They sing and they dance as they come closer to gigantic flames that reach the sky. After all, it's Simhat Torah and they must celebrate the eternity of Israel, and wait for the Messiah, whose idea of eternity—but not of Israel—must be different from theirs.

Lublin, during the darkest hours, became a center for torment and death. Lublin, an ingathering place for condemned Jews, led to nearby Belzec. Lublin meant Majdanek. Lublin meant the great fall not of one man, nor of one people, but of mankind.

And yet, and yet . . .

What do we learn from all this? We learn that the tale of Lublin survives Lublin, that the beauty of Lublin is mightier than Lublin. We learn that what the Tzaddik may do, the Hasid is not permitted to do. The Master may come close to despair, his followers may not. Hasidism is a movement out of despair, away from despair—a movement against despair. Only Hasidism? Judaism too. Who is a Jew? A Jew is he—or she—whose song cannot be muted, nor can his or her joy be killed by the enemy . . . ever.

# Rebbe Naphtali
# of Ropshitz

It happened on Shabbat-Hagadol—the one that precedes Passover, which is an important holiday, though . . . a costly one. It requires money, a great deal of money, to celebrate it the way it should be celebrated. Yet the people of Ropshitz had none, or almost none. There were but a few rich merchants; all the others lived from day to day, worrying about each penny, each mouthful that they brough back home. The men were constantly overworked, so were the women. Even the children were pale with fatigue and hunger. That was the picture all year around—which was bad enough. But the week before Passover it became even worse. For at Passover, every Jew must consider himself free and sovereign—free of worries and bonds—like a king.

So on this particular Shabbat, the rabbi of the community—Rebbe Naphtali—devotes his speech to the theme of *tzedakah*—charity. He quotes parables, invokes the authority of Talmudic sages, adds argument to argument, asking those who are well-off to share with the have-nots, the victims of heaven, the deprived ones, so as not to embarrass them at the Seder, when through the open door the Prophet Elijah will enter and be their guest of honor.

On no other holiday is food so important—on no other holiday is money so important.

Rebbe Naphtali explains, argues, pleads, orders. Never before has he spoken with such ardor; never before has he put his entire soul into every one of his words. For this was the time of year when the poor felt even poorer. He *had* to bring them some joy for the holiday. He *had* to succeed in convincing his congregation—he *had* to, at any price.

Back home, after services, he falls into a chair, exhausted. His wife asks him how it went. Were there many people? Yes, many; the place was packed. Did so-and-so attend? Yes. And such-and-such? Also. Did you speak? Yes. Were you good? Yes, I believe so. Did you succeed in convincing them? With a smile, Rebbe Naphtali answers: "I only half succeeded, and that isn't too bad." And as the woman seems not to understand, he explains: "I convinced the poor to receive—but not the rich to give."

Original, picturesque, amusing, Rebbe Naphtali is a friend, an equal, of the greatest—with a difference: he dares to antagonize the holy Seer of Lublin, who dislikes his sense of humor, and Rebbe Mendel of Riminov, who distrusts his political views. He even dares respectfully to mock the founder of a school, the revered Rebbe Elimelekh of Lizensk. He is Hasidism's *enfant terrible*. Other Masters speak of God; he discusses everyday down-to-earth matters. Other Rebbes cry; he laughs. Better yet: he makes people laugh. Others tend to take life seriously, if not tragically; there are but few things *he* takes seriously. Laughter is one of them. "Why do you laugh while I am crying?" asked Rebbe Mendel of Riminov.—"Because you are crying while I am laughing," he replied. For him, laughter performs a philosophical, quasi-religious function. With him, laughter becomes an integral part of Hasidic experience and its tales.

Another story:

The celebrated Rebbe Israel, Maggid of Kozhenitz, was said to have such powers that he could be denied nothing in the higher spheres. When the request was simple, he would close his eyes and whisper a prayer. When the request was more difficult to fulfill, he would include it in his thoughts during services. But the most complicated cases he would take up late, very late, at night, surrounded by silence and solitude. For each midnight, sitting on the floor, his forehead covered with ashes, he would mourn over the destruction of the Temple, whose flames still flickered in his eyes, and he would cry with such intense sorrow that it became impossible—up there—not to lend him an ear. His tears would open all the gates. And then, in the midst of his litanies, he would quickly slip in an urgent plea for this one rotting away in prison, or this one with a dying wife, or a heartbroken old maid—and all his wishes would be granted. And he knew it. And he was pleased.

Only once did he encounter a refusal. On that particular night his pleas were not accepted. His prayers were returned; his tears had no effect in heaven. Unhappy, he demanded an explanation. When he received it, he understood—and forgave.

For that same night Rebbe Naphtali of Ropshitz had been on the road, on his way to Kozhenitz. In the inn where he had stopped to rest, a wedding was in full swing; the men and women were drinking and eating and singing. Only the bride was sad, terribly sad. Rebbe Naphtali, who was traveling incognito, wanted to console her.

"Why are you sad?" he asked her.

"Because," she answered, "there is something missing in this wedding, something essential to make it festive and joyous. A jester! There is no jester here to make us laugh—that's why I am sad."

"Is that all?" the Rebbe cried out. "Then stop being sad! For the heavens, may they be blessed, have foreseen this possibility. They have sent me here tonight to dispel your sadness, for I am a *badkhan* by profession, a troubadour and jester—a wedding specialist!"

And he began to compose rhymes about the company, the innkeeper, the rabbi and the cantor, and he did it with so much talent, so much humor, that all the guests fell under his spell and responded by laughing loud and hard. And the bride, too, was amused. To make her even happier, he sang with great exuberance and told funny stories—and danced—and danced. All around the table the guests were shaking with laughter, and up there, in paradise, the sages and the saints, sitting around their Master and ours, interrupted their studies and listened, and laughed, and laughed. And the angels forgot their nocturnal missions and flapped their wings and laughed, and laughed. And in the palace of the celestial tribunal, the judges stopped judging and sentencing, for the prosecutor had stopped prosecuting, and they, too, could not resist laughter. The Supreme Judge Himself stopped receiving His servants' prayers and litanies, including the tears of the holy Maggid of Kozhenitz—for He, too, was listening to the funny stories of Rebbe Naphtali. And He, too, was laughing, He was laughing . . .

Later the Maggid of Kozhenitz would say to his friend and disciple: "Naphtali, Naphtali, are you aware of your own strength? What I cannot accomplish with my tears, you accomplish with laughter!"


Rebbe Naphtali of Ropshitz was born in 1760, in Linsk, a hamlet in Galicia, the very same day that Rebbe Israel Baal Shem Tov died at Medzebozh.

Simple coincidence perhaps? Hasidism denies coincidences. No event is isolated, no encounter deprived of meaning. Some disciples insinuated that, on a very high level, Rebbe Naphtali was the Besht's successor. It is quite possible, since the same could be said—and was—of all great Masters. Except that these particular two personalities had few traits in common: if the Besht was the perfect Master, Rebbe Naphtali was the perfect disciple.

His father, a noted Talmudist, served as local rabbi and was rather hostile to Hasidism. Not so his mother; she was the one who turned little Naphtali into a Hasid. At thirteen, for his bar mitzvah, he went with her to the great Rebbe Mekhal of Zlotchov, a disciple of the Besht and a companion of the Mezeritcher Maggid. Rebbe Mekhal was the one who helped him put on the tephillin for the first time, and remarked: "I have just tied his soul up there; the knot will be a lasting one."

Shortly thereafter Naphtali was engaged to the daughter of a wealthy Jew, a wine merchant, from Brodi. The marriage created a sensation—though less than the divorce that followed one year later. The reason? One day he came home and found his young wife primping in front of a mirror. "Don't," he said; "I like you the way you are." — "And the others don't count?" she answered. Troubled by such impudence, he fled from the house and took refuge with the Rebbe of Zlotchov, having already made up his mind to divorce.

When he remarried—a year later—he settled in Ropshitz as official rabbi. Was he happier with his second wife? A witness, Rebbe Yekhezkel of Shinev, says no. And I quote: "Rebbe Naphtali of Ropshitz had the rare and awesome powers to bring the Messiah, but couldn't use them—he was prevented by heaven; he was given as a wife a woman who disturbed him, bored him and annoyed him."

She would often boast about her own erudition and piety, and remarked once that her father regretted that she was born a girl and not a boy, for then his son would have become the greatest of the great scholars alive. "In this case I agree with your father," said Rebbe Naphtali. "I also regret that you were not born a boy."

Was it because he spent so little time at home that she made his life miserable? Or was it, on the contrary, she who made him stay away so much? The fact remains that it was easier to meet him in other people's homes than in his own. Though he was the rabbi of his town, and later also of his native town, where he inherited his father's position, he managed to assume and fulfill his official functions in both places—and at the same time roam around the capitals of the Hasidic universe.

He spent one year at the court of Rebbe Mordekhai of Neshkhiz. Then he spent some time with Rebbe Elimelekh of Lizensk, who at first refused to accept him as disciple: "I don't want VIPs in my house," he said. Crushed, the young Naphtali stretched out on the floor and began to shed bitter tears and even to spit blood: "Is it my fault that my father is rabbi?" he cried. The Tzaddik of Lizensk finally gave in.

But these were brief attachments. Others, more lasting, linked him to the Seer of Lublin, the Maggid of Kozhenitz, and Reb Mendel of Riminov. He sought their company; he admired them, all three of them, and all at once, as though to contradict the Lizensker theories of exclusivity. He, Naphtali of Ropshitz, demonstrated that one could have ties to more than one Master; that one could believe in more than one Tzaddik. He believed this so strongly that, while they were alive, he refused to serve as Rebbe himself.

All three died the same year: 1815–1816. He himself died in 1827. In other words, his reign lasted but ten years. Time enough to leave a mark on the life, the ways, and the language of Hasidism.

Time enough, also, to attract and keep disciples such as Rebbe Haim of Czanz and Rebbe Sholem of Kaminka. They could frequently be found in his kitchen . . . peeling potatoes. Reb Haim would say about him: "I never called him Rebbe, for I didn't learn anything from him. I couldn't. He was too profound for me. All I took from him . . . is *yiraat shamayim*, fear of heaven."

Ten years—time enough to make himself enemies as well. Both inside and outside the Hasidic movement. The Mitnagdim—the adversaries—made his life so miserable that he predicted their punishment: after their death they would all return, reincarnated as dogs. Inside the movement, his principal enemy was Reb Shlomo-Leib of Lentsheno. But as Hasidic quarrels go, this one was neither too serious nor too fierce. He suffered but didn't show it. Answering his critics, he quoted the biblical phrase: "And the Jews were jealous of both Moses and Aaron"; they resented Moses' solitude and Aaron's sociability. Impossible to please everybody.

Yet he had fewer adversaries, fewer rivals, fewer enemies than most Masters. Even among the Tzaddikim of faraway dynasties, his prestige was great. The Rizhiner praised his intelligence and so did the Premishlaner, and even the Pshiskher. He was invited to all the courts, to all the festivities; he earned his peers' loyalty by being loyal to them—all of them. He saw himself not as prince but as messenger, as link between the various Rebbes.

If two Rebbes were rivals or enemies, that was no reason for Rebbe Naphtali not to befriend both . . . and he did. Most leaders sought his allegiance, for they considered him not only a valuable friend, but also a man of wisdom. In Hasidic literature he is most often described as a wise man—wisdom is his trademark. "Rebbe Naphtali is a *hokhem*," they would say.

A peculiar description? He had others as well. Cheerful, lucky, optimist. Frequently in trouble because of his humor—and always saved by his humor. He loved to tease the Masters he admired. When the Rizhiner paid him a compliment, expecting some words of protest—he did not protest. The Maggid of Kozhenitz, eternally ill, goes to the *mikvah?* Rebbe Naphtali slips into his bed. Rebbe Elimelekh insists on maintaining an hour of isolation between *Minha* and *Maariv?* Rebbe Naphtali hides *under* the bed. If that isn't enough, he dares to imitate him in public: leaning on his cane the way he does, concentrating the way he does and even distributing blessings to followers in distress . . . the way he does. Strangely enough, Rebbe Elimelekh—known for his temper—lets him get away with it. "Aha," he says, "I see you have learned my tricks."

Rebbe Naphtali got away with worse offenses. Perhaps because they were not directed against any one Tzaddik in particular, but against all. He was and was not one of them. Other Rebbes attract admirers by offering them miracles? He offers no miracles and wants no admirers. He says: "Rebbes usually pray that people should come to see them and be helped. I pray that they should be helped at home."

And . . . he is forgiven. Forgiven his skeptical comments, his sharp remarks. Forgiven his way of gently mocking his own peers, and their habit of taking money for their services. Invited to spend Shabbat at Vielipol, he asks a fee: twenty coins. They promise to pay—and don't. They can't. So he demands the synagogue's chandelier be taken down and given to him. Does he need it? Or take it? Of course not; this is his way of refusing all fees. A visitor asks him: "We are told that the universe was created six thousand years ago, yet astronomers claim that there exists one star which is visible once every thirty-six thousand years!" — "So what?" says the Rebbe. "God can be found in this mystery too. Look for Him—not for the star."

He is forgiven everything—because of his humor. Furthermore, his wit is directed at the Establishment and not at the followers. He loves Rebbes and loves Hasidim, and wants to be both—and serve as bridge between them.

"For a long time I refused the role of leader," said he, "because a Rebbe must flatter his followers. I had thought of becoming a tailor, a cobbler, a street sweeper, a bath attendant, even a beadle. And then I realized that the tailor, too, must flatter his customer. And so must the beadle. And the cobbler. So . . . I might as well join the rabbinate."

Even as Rebbe, he adopted an attitude of amused sobriety toward himself. One day he remarked: "In the more distant provinces I am called Rebbe Naphtali of Ropshitz. In Ropshitz, where I am well known, I am referred to as the Rebbe of Ropshitz. But my wife, who knows me best, simply calls me Naphtali." He himself preferred the surname Naphtali *der Belfer*—the tutor.

His very first sermon in Ropshitz made a stir. It is customary on Shabbat that the speaker take into account three principles: the speech must be true, brief, and linked to the Sidra of the week. "Well," he said, "I confess I don't know what portion is being read this week." This is true, brief, and to the point. End of speech.

(His practical advice to preachers: Make the introduction concise and the conclusion abrupt—with nothing in between.)

Another time he ascended the bimah, the podium. It was Shabbat-Shuva, between Rosh Hashana and Yom Kippur. For what seemed a long time, he silently stared at the congregation. Then he said: "What is man? A worm of the earth—and yet you fear his words." And once more he came down from the bimah without another word.

But his strong point was not sermons but conversation. His sense of humor was direct, concrete, and showed a swift and sharp mind. Every one of his words hit home.

Even as a child, he baffled adults with his quick replies. A visitor, a friend of his father, turned to him one day: "Naphtali . . . if you tell me where God can be found, I'll give you a golden coin." —Answered the child: "And I'll give you two if you tell me where He can *not* be found."

A Hasid implored him to intercede in heaven on his behalf, saying: "I study, I learn Torah day and night, and I do not make any progress; I still don't know it." —"God didn't ask you to *know* His law, but to study it," was the Rebbe's reply.

Another Hasid, wishing to repent, came to see him. With a story, a classic story. About a friend who committed all the sins enumerated by Torah: sins against God, sins against man, and against himself. But now the friend saw the light, repented, and would like to know what to do to expiate his sins. But he is timid and doesn't dare to come himself. "What advice would you give him?" —"He should have come and said that he was speaking not for himself but for his friend," was the Rebbe's tongue-in-cheek reply.

Once, while going around collecting funds to ransom prisoners, he arrived in a small village where there lived a Jew known for his money and for his unwillingness to part with it. Fearing the rhetorical talents of the Rebbe, this Jew hid in the hayloft, under huge bundles of hay. Knowing his man, the Ropshitzer went straight to the hiding place. Face to face with the embarrassed miser, he had this sublime word: "The Talmud claims that to offer hospitality is a deed more important that welcoming the Shekhina. I never understood why; now I do. To welcome the Shekhina, Moses covered his face. You, when you receive guests, cover your entire body."

He hated misers—he hated them almost as much as fools and hypocrites. Hypocrisy was to him the most degrading of sins. He loved to expose fakers. Nothing made him happier than to unmask self-styled ascetics who wanted only to impress, to show off. "Life is given to man to be lived," he

109

would say. "To mutilate life is to offend its source; to choose suffering is to reject a gift both rare and irreplaceable. The path to paradise leads through the world of reality," he maintained.

He, incidentally, displayed but a very qualified interest in paradise. He affirmed without the slightest hesitation: "Better to go to hell with wise men than to paradise with fools." The Seer of Lublin reproached him with attaching too much importance to intelligence. This is what he answered: "Yes, it is true that the Torah orders man to be naïve, or whole—*tamim*—with God. Only, to be naïve, one must be *very* intelligent." On another occasion he said: "Three principal virtues enable man to comprehend and communicate truth. They are: kindness, devotion and intelligence. Kindness alone leads to promiscuity; devotion alone comes close to stupidity; intelligence alone is conducive to crime. So it is essential that the three qualities be present together for man to benefit from them." Well, he possessed them all. But above all, he was known for his cleverness, wit, and intelligence.

However, a question arises: What made him so clever? What exactly did his intelligence consist of? In his two posthumous collections we read his comments on Torah, we repeat his amusing anecdotes. We smile, we laugh—but we do not cry out in wonder. We are struck neither by the depth of his perception nor by his erudition. On the contrary, his metaphors, though brilliant, lack the anguish of a

Kotzker saying and the fire of a Bratzlaver tale. Where is his *hokhma,* his wisdom, of which one speaks so much in Hasidic literature? In that he managed to serve several Masters at once without arousing their jealousy? Because he enjoyed himself and enjoyed practical jokes? Because he possessed common sense, a talent for practical living . . . and making friends?

We should like to know his definition of *hokhma.* Unfortunately, it was either not formulated or not transmitted. Was it wisdom? Cleverness? Shrewdness? Intuition? We know only this: that every time his wisdom was mentioned he replied with some witty line. As though to prove that he did not take it seriously. The word provoked a strange reflex in his behavior, a reflex totally unrelated to the subject matter.

One day the Rizhiner turned to him: "You are considered a sage. So tell us a story." And Rebbe Naphtali obeyed. He told a story, a terrible story, how a long time ago he had deceived a notorious village miser by impersonating the son-in-law of Rabbi Meir Baal-hanés, husband of Brourya and a famous miracle-maker of the second century of the common time. Fooled, the villager gave him money, which he, the Ropshitzer, and his companions, used to purchase some . . . *yash*—liquor. Could that be a mark of wisdom and compassion to mistreat the fellow, no matter how ignorant? No matter how miserly? More surprising is the Rizhiner's com-

111

ment: "I knew that you were a sage—but not like this!" And both burst out laughing. What were they laughing about? At whose expense?

It is easier to see his mind work when he meets younger or simpler people. Except that . . . to them he lost. He himself would often say that he had lost three verbal encounters.

The first time he lost to his son, the future Rebbe Eliezer of Dzhikov. Seeing him play one day, Rebbe Naphtali scolded him for wasting precious time, time he could have put to better use—to study Torah, for instance. "It's not my fault," said the little boy. "It's the fault of the *yetzer-hara*, the evil spirit. It's he who led me into sin." — "Well answered, son," said the father. "But you should follow the example of the *yetzer-hara;* even he, by inducing you to sin, does obey God's will. Why don't you do likewise?" —"For him it's easy," said the little boy. "The *yetzer-hara* has no *yetzer-hara* to influence him against obeying God's will!"

The second time he was defeated by a little girl. He had met her in a small village with some ten Jewish inhabitants. Still, it did have a synagogue and a cemetery. "I don't understand," said the Rebbe to the little girl. "Either the cemetery or the synagogue is superfluous. If one of the ten men dies, there will be no more services in the synagogue. If no one dies, what's the cemetery for?" — "Don't worry," said the little girl. "The synagogue will remain open. As for the cemetery, it's for strangers."

The third defeat was inflicted upon him by a coachman. It was on Simhat Torah Eve. The Hasidim were rejoicing, celebrating—as one should—the presence and sanctity of the Torah by dancing to the point of drunkenness, by singing to the point of ecstasy. Suddenly the Ropshitzer saw in the middle of the crowd a coachman who was known for his primitive way of life and ignorance. "What!" the Rebbe cried out. "You participate in the festivity? You who never study Torah, you who obey its commandments so badly and so rarely? How does this festivity concern you?" And the coachman replied: "Rebbe, Rebbe, if my brother arranges a wedding, a bar mitzvah, or any other celebration, am I not allowed to participate?

This anecdote, which seems cruel, damages him, not the coachman. Yet he himself told it. To show that the coachman was right—that the coachman had a better understanding of things than he.

For this complex and complicated Tzaddik was, in spite of appearances, profoundly humble—and sad. But his humility was hidden under arrogance and pride, just as his melancholy was covered with exuberance.

It is told that one night he was surprised by a visitor from his village who found him sitting on the ground, his face bathed in tears, lamenting the destruction of the Temple in Jerusalem. Yet, lest the visitor take him for a hidden saint, he began to indulge in self-glorification: "Oh," he said aloud, "if

113

the Jews of Ropshitz only knew the true qualities, the rare greatness of their Rebbe!" He wanted people to take him for a vain person, a comedian, rather than a Just Man.

He loved to comment on the passage in Talmud in which God showed Moses *"Dor dor vedorshav"*— all the future generations and their leaders. "Why," he asked, "did God not start with the leaders? This is why: because of the regression in history. The closer we come to our times, the less striking are the leaders. Imagine Moses resting his gaze on me. He would undoubtedly cry out: 'What! Naphtali, too, is a Rebbe?' But since God would by then have shown him my contemporaries, Moses would understand: 'All right, let it be. He, too, can be a leader . . . alas!' "

He was harsh on them, harsh on himself.

To understand him better, we must analyze his attachment to his favorite *mitzvah:* that of *succah.* Like the Berditchever, he said that his very soul was rooted in that commandment. Not one day went by without his mentioning something connected with Succoth, the Feast of the Huts, which lasts only one week. This attachment is symbolic. What is a *succah?* Half tent, half hut, a temporary refuge whose one side remains constantly exposed to rains and winds. It is small, modest, and austere—it reminds us of our life in the desert and not in the royal palace in Jerusalem.

Rebbe Naphtali's obsession with Succoth offers the first clue to his hidden image. Only someone who dwells in the desert seeks a tent with such intensity. To rest. To breathe. To dream. What is the *succah* if not the Temple of Jerusalem before Jerusalem—the vision before fulfillment? Only a nostalgic and unhappy visionary could live year-round in his own private *succah*.

The Ropshitzer—sad? Unhappy? He whose gaiety was as legendary as was the Kotzker's depression? People saw his laughter but not the torment beneath it; he ranks among the most misunderstood figures in Hasidism.

That is what he wanted: not to be understood. Not to be pitied. He concealed his pain—and that was his wisdom. He laughed so as not to cry; he chose exhibitionism so as to hide his anguish, his lack of confidence in himself, in his own powers, in his own words.

One Shabbat, surrounded by his followers, he delivered an impressive address. Everyone listened with bated breath. Whoever was present rose with him to the highest spheres of mystical meditation. Everything he discovered became visible, and one could witness creation. After Shabbat was over, Rebbe Naphtali ran to his friend and teacher Reb Mendel of Riminov. "I'm afraid," he said, "I'm afraid I spoke too well; I must have said things I shouldn't have . . ." Reb Mendel asked him to repeat

115

the address, so he could judge for himself. And I like to believe that Rebbe Naphtali invented— improvised—another lecture on the spot.

Was he consoled? Comforted? If so, it didn't last long. It never did. From his early youth he lacked self-confidence, to the point of soliciting blessings from everyone, even from strangers. Nobody as yet knew The Jew of Pshiskhe when Naphtali Ropshitzer had already asked his blessings.

To his disciple Reb Yehuda-Zvi of Razdal he said: "One day you will be Rebbe. You will have to offer blessings to people. So start with me." The disciple refused. "You are wrong," insisted the Ropshitzer. "You see, when I was your age, the great Levi-Yitzhak of Berditchev pleaded with me for the same favor, and I also refused. And I regret it to this day."

Behind the visible Ropshitzer, there was another—invisible—one. The first told stories, teased the great and amused them; the second, withdrawn in his own inner tent, lived in silence and torment, aspiring to attain some unattainable truth.

In other words: there were *two* Naphtali Ropshitzer. The first was playing a game so as to conceal the other.

The first was active, militant, gay, exuberant— singing the praises of hope and life in the best tradition of the Baal Shem Tov. His very presence drove away sadness. With one funny remark he disarmed depression; with one word he brought joy. No matter what the cost, the unhappy Jews in Galicia, who had nobody but their Rebbe in the whole world, needed to laugh, to rejoice, to hold on to existence. In this respect, the Ropshitzer performed a vital function: his combat against despair was a personal one. He didn't trust disciples or messengers; he came alone wherever communities in distress were in danger of giving in to resignation. His weapons? Song and laughter.

One evening of Simhat Torah the news arrives that his friend and disciple, Reb Avraham of Oulanov, had died. The Hasidim don't have the heart to go on with the festivities. So he scolds them angrily: "Are we not at war—at war with destiny, with the entire world? What does one do at the front when an officer falls? What does one do? Does one run away? On the contrary, one closes ranks and fights even harder. So close your ranks and dance, dance, with more vigor than ever; dance like you have never danced before!"

On another occasion he remarked: "What is a Hasid? Someone who possesses a precious key, a key that opens all the doors, even those that God keeps closed. And that key is . . . the *Nigoun*, the song of joy that makes our hearts thrill. The *Nigoun* opens the gates of heaven. Melancholy closes them."

Dynamic, tireless, the visible Tzaddik participates in Hasidic life. He encourages, he mediates, he entertains wherever his talents are needed. He visits all the courts to bring them closer to each

117

other. Rather than repudiate the society surrounding him, he works on it from the inside. He says: "What is the difference between the Prophet and the Tzaddik? The Prophet unveils the future—and the Tzaddik the present. His task is the more difficult."

Yet he himself accomplishes it. He is the wandering minstrel who brings smiles to poor children and memories to their old, tired grandparents. In the famous quarrel between Lublin and Pshiskhe, he urges moderation, and fails; though not publicly, he opposes the messianic conspiracy of his three friends; he is against suffering and war—against using them for any purpose, be it the most sacred of all.

The conspiracy failed and the three Masters died in the same year. It was Rebbe Naphtali who saw to the holy Seer's burial. Dressed as gravedigger, his clothes covered with mud, he buried him in Lublin, whispering: "This is how one looks when one buries one's teacher."

He always found the right word for every situation. But behind words, there are other words, inaudible, imperceptible words, and behind them, there is silence.

There was silence in Rebbe Naphtali.


This is a parable he loved to retell: One day the Czar, while inspecting his troops at the front, fails to notice an enemy soldier whose rifle is aimed at him. Fortunately for the Czar, one of his loyal soldiers pulls the imperial horse's reins and so averts tragedy. The grateful Czar asks his savior: "Tell me your secret wish and consider it granted."—"Majesty," says the soldier, "my corporal is cruel; send him to another company."—"Fool," the Czar cries out. "Why don't you ask to be made corporal yourself?"

Man's tragedy lies not in the refusal but in his inability to desire. He demands too little; he no longer lifts his eyes to lofty summits; his dreams drag in the dust and his words are empty. That is the discovery Rebbe Naphtali may have made toward the end of his life.

Did he regret his past? Would he have liked to choose another way? Possibly. He had tried it once upon a time, in his youth, when he sought truth in ascetic modes such as rolling naked in the snow or prolonged fasting. He had given it up—as a Hasid, he had to. Now it was too late to start all over again. The traveler had reached the end of his journey. The singer felt no more desire to confront his audience. The troubadour was tired. Now it was the *other* Ropshitzer who emerged and dominated.

Rebbe Naphtali went into seclusion. He stopped entertaining, stopped visiting Rebbes and receiving their admirers; he turned away from his own followers and now retired into his own beloved, invisible, and haunted *succah*—between four walls. Surprisingly and symbolically, he stopped speaking.

For months and months no word left his lips.

To the questions of his son, Reb Eliezer of Dzhikev, he opposed absolute silence. In the beginning he would explain by gestures that his muteness was due to fatigue, to exhaustion, and ought not be mystically interpreted. Later he stopped explaining altogether. He remained silent. Alone.

Then came the last day. The sick father and his son are alone.

"Speak, Father," begs Reb Eliezer. "Say something, one word." The old Master looks at him and says nothing. "You can," pleads the son, "I know you can; you can speak. Why don't you? Why don't you want to speak, Father?"

The old Master stares at him for a long, long moment and then replies in a slow, burning whisper: "I . . . am . . . afraid. Do you . . . understand? Do you understand, Eliezer? I. Am. Afraid."

Afraid of what? Of whom? We shall never know.

But he did.

*These great Masters whom we have just encountered, it is with reluctance that the story-teller considers leaving them; their hold on him has never been stronger.*

*Such is the power of their legends; their intense and moving beauty stays with you and involves you. A Hasidic story is about Hasidim more than about their Masters; it is about those who retell it as much as about those who experienced it.*

*How can the attraction they held for their contemporaries be comprehended today? Close to God, they were also close to those who were seeking Him. They were endowed with mystical powers and they used them not to isolate themselves from their communities, but rather to penetrate them more deeply.*

*Inspired, they became a source of inspiration. They communicated joy and fervor to men and women who needed joy and fervor to live and even to survive. In a cold and hostile world they incarnated a powerful call to hope and friendship.*

*Friendship: a key word in Hasidic vocabulary.* Dibuk-haverim *for the disciple is as important as*

Emunat-tzadikim, *faith in the Master. To follow a certain Rebbe means to relate to his pupils. A Hasid alone is not a true Hasid. Solitude and Hasidism are incompatible. What was the Hasidic movement in its origins if not a protest against solitude? The villager tore himself away from his farm, from his daily misery and uncertainties, and went to spend the High Holidays, or a simple Sabbath, with his Rebbe—not just to see and hear him and be with him but also to meet his companions, his friends. To celebrate with them. To pray with them. And dream with them.*

*And yet, and yet . . . all these Masters who moved others to joy, to new heights of ecstasy, seemed to struggle with melancholy and at times even with despair.*

*The Baal Shem Tov himself was not spared. Sometimes, especially toward the end of his life, he appeared overwhelmed, subdued. As did his successor, the celebrated Maggid of Mezeritch. And Rebbe Elimelekh of Lizensk. And Rebbe Nahman of Bratzlav. In all of them a common obsession emerges: to combat sorrow with exuberance, to overcome despair with prayer, to defeat resignation by kindling a greater light, a more exalted faith in God and in His creation.*

*Intercessor rather than intermediary (the Jewish tradition rejects the concept of intermediaries in the relations of man to God), the Master often cannot but feel inadequate: all these vigils, all these prayers, all these promises, all these appeals, and the Messiah who does not come. All these sufferings, all these trials, and heaven remains closed. And the Shekhina is still in exile. And so* is the Jewish people. What must one do to keep from going under, what can one do? Said Rebbe Aaron of Karlin: "Either God is God and I do not do enough to serve Him, or He is not and then it is my fault." The exile and its darkness, whose fault is it? The hatred, the torment, the enemies, who is to blame? Hunger, thirst, death: how is one to accept them? The Master listens to his followers' tales of woe and cannot escape despair.

But he controls himself, and overcoming all obstacles—reasons, reality, doubt, irony—liberates in himself and in his followers a certain kind of joy that will be justified only retroactively. He creates happiness so as not to yield to unhappiness. He tells stories so as to escape the temptation of silence.

To express my admiration and my love for them would be repetitious. But then repetition is part of the Hasidic tradition. In the school of Bratzlav, for example, disciples and their students tell the tales of Rebbe Nahman a thousand times, and each time they discover some new meaning, some new wonder. So do we.

In retelling these tales, I realize once more that I owe them much. Consciously or not, I have incorporated a song, an echo, a word of theirs in my own legends and fables. I have remained, in a vanished kingdom, a child who loves to listen.

Elsewhere, I imagined a man who one day finds himself sharing a cell with a madman. After a while, he feels his reason failing; he knows that he is going to lose it completely. Exposed to madness, he will ultimately become its victim. And so, in order not to go mad, he sets out to cure his mad cell-mate. *Were the hero of my tale but aware, would he have understood that he was only following in the steps of the Hasidic Masters who, in this volume, I have tried to evoke?*

*Earlier I mentioned that the story-teller was soon to leave them. Forgive him: he will not. For even if he wanted to, he could not; they surely would not agree to recede into the shadows of his memory.*

*More than ever, we, the living, need to imagine them alive.*

# Background Notes

*Amidah* (literally "standing"): Also known as the *Shemoneh Esre* (literally "the eighteen"). Obligatory prayer consisting of a series of blessings and recited while standing during every service.

*beadle:* The equivalent in the synagogue to a church sexton.

*Beit Midrash* (literally "House of Study"): In order not to interrupt meditation and discussion on the Sacred Word, the rabbinical academics chose to remain there for services rather than move to the Beit Knesseth, the assembly house (synagogue). The two "Houses" often became one, or at least were made to adjoin, with services extending into study and study culminating in prayer.

*Baal Shem* (literally "Master of the Name"): Title attributed since the Middle Ages to men who know the true name of beings and things, recognize their secret, and can act upon them and through them. By naming the forces, such a man masters them; his knowledge is power. Were he to use this power to attain immediate or profane gains, he would be nothing

125

more than a miracle-maker. But if he chooses to bring the names closer to the Name and unite beings and things with God, he becomes Master of the Good Name, Baal Shem Tov.

*The Besht:* Rebbe Israel Baal Shem Tov (1700–1760). The Founder of the Hasidic movement.

*challah:* White, braided bread eaten on Shabbat.

*Gog and Magog:* The opponents of the Messiah. In the great eschatological battle against the righteous host, they are to head the forces of evil. In rabbinic literature, the rebel people who rise up against God and His anointed.

*Hasid* (literally fervent, pious): One who acts out of love, with tenderness. Derived from *hesed,* grace, one of God's attributes complementing *din,* strict justice. God's grace calls forth the fervor, the piety of man, his love for God and all His creatures.

In the Psalms, *Hasid* (pl., *Hasidim*) often denotes the "faithful," the "lover of God." In Mishnah the Hasid is described as one who is slow to anger and quick to relent, who gives freely himself and urges others to do the same, as indicated by the phrase, "What is mine is yours and what is yours is yours also" (Avot 5:13). The Talmud identifies a Hasid as one "who, even before he prays, turns his heart to God—for at least one hour" (Ber. 30b). And Hasidim are even to be found among Gentiles: "The Hasidim among the Gentiles will have their share in the world to come" (T. Sanh. 13; Mishne Torah, Melakim 11).

In the second century B.C.E. a Jewish sect, the Hasidim or Assideans, "valiant men whose hearts were bound to the Law" (1 Macc. 2:42), fought with the Maccabees against Antiochus Epiphanus. But refusing all compromise on religious laws and unwilling to become involved in politics, they broke away from the Hasmononean dynasty after victory had been achieved. The Talmud refers to them as "the Hasidim of yore."

In the thirteenth century of the Common Era, there flourished in the Rhineland an important school called the Hasidim of Ashkenaz, the "Holy Men of Germany." They created a trend of thought that found wide acceptance. Their major work, the *Sefer Hasidim*, the "Book of the Devout," rooted in Jewish mystical tradition, stresses the majesty of God but also the mystery of oneness, elaborating a veritable philosophy of history and man's relationship to man, emphasizing the importance of silent piety, of prayer, and of a system of ethics based on renunciation of earthly matters, spiritual serenity, and total love of one's fellow man that culminates in the expression of the fear and the love of God in "the joy that scorches the heart."

*heder:* An elementary religious school of the type prevalent in Eastern Europe, often situated in a single room in the teacher's home.

*Maariv:* Evening service, also called "arevit," recited daily after nightfall and named after one of the opening words of its first prayer.

*maggid:* A popular preacher. The maggid became a characteristic feature of the Russian and Polish Jewish communities. From the seventeenth century on, the rabbis preached only twice a year; preaching throughout the rest of the year was left to the maggid. It was mainly by means of wandering preachers that Hasidim was spread in the eighteenth century.

*maskilim:* A title of honor for a learned man.

*melamed:* A teacher who ran the single-room heder.

*mikvah:* Ritual bath for immersion to wash every uncleanness.

*Minhah:* The second of the two statutory daily services. It is recited anytime during the afternoon until sunset and corresponds to the daily "evening" sacrifice in the Temple.

*Mishnah* (literally "study"): Compendia of tradition compiled in Palestine ca. 200 C.E.

*Mitnagdim* (literally "adversaries"): They opposed the "new Hasidic sect," in the eighteenth and nineteenth centuries, judging it revolutionary, dangerous, heretical.

*Queen Shabbat:* The Sabbath is welcomed as a bride and a queen and the end of the Sabbath is marked by a festive meal *Melavveh Malkah*—"accompanying the Queen."

*Rabbi:* Literally "master" or "teacher."

*Reb:* Mr.

*Rebbe:* Term used for Hasidic leaders and spiritual guides. The Rebbe or Tzaddik is not necessarily a halakhic scholar and teacher, but guides his followers by virtue of his spiritual power and holiness.

*Shabbat:* The Sabbath, the weekly day of rest, observed from sunset of Friday until nightfall Saturday.

*Shavuoth:* Holiday in late spring, commemorating the gift of Torah at Mount Sinai.

*Shekhina:* The Divine Presence. Tradition has it that the radiance of the Shekhina with its many blessings accompanies those who are pious and righteous.

*shohet:* One trained and ordained to perform the ritual slaughter used to supply kosher meats.

*Shulkhan Arukh:* A compendium of Jewish Law compiled in the sixteenth century C.E. by Joseph Caro.

*Simhat Torah:* Festival of the Law in the autumn; the last day of Succoth celebrating the end of the yearly cycle of reading the Torah.

*shtetl:* A very small town.

*shtibl:* House of Prayer of Hasidim, usually extremely small with only one or two rooms.

*succah:* A temporary, wooden hut covered with branches, in which all meals are taken during Succoth.

*Succoth:* Feast of Tabernacles; begins four days after Yom Kippur.

*Talmud* (literally "learning"): Mishnah plus Gemara, the commentary on the Mishnah produced in rabbinical academies from ca. 200–500 C.E.

## Background Notes

*Torah* (literally "teaching"): Can refer to the Pentateuch, or to all of Scripture, or to all revelation, written or oral, in Judaism.

*tephillin:* Phylacteries; two leather cases which are bound by straps attached to the forehead and the left arm during the morning prayer.

*Tzaddik:* Just Man, ideal of moral, social and religious perfection. He is a man "who lives by his faith," and to whom God responds. In the Hasidic movement the Tzaddik rapidly became an institution, but though a "spiritual model," when exposed to temptation, he was not always able to resist, going as far as to proclaim himself intermediary between his disciples and God, presiding over veritable courts and founding dynasties.

*Zohar:* The "Book of Splendor," principal work of Kabbala, esoteric commentary on the Pentateuch, traditionally attributed to Rabbi Shimon Bar-Yohai.

# Synchronology

| | | IN THE JEWISH WORLD |
|---|---|---|

| | 1720 | 1720 In Lowicz (Poland), the clergy decides to prohibit the building of new and the restoration of old synagogues.<br>1727 First Jews naturalized in American colonies. |
|---|---|---|
| **Pinhas of Koretz**<br>**(1728–1791)** | | |
| | 1730 | 1730 Founding of the first synagogue in New York.<br>1738 Public execution in Stuttgart of Joseph Susskind Oppenheimer (Jud Süss). |
| | 1740 | |
| **The Seer of Lublin**<br>**(1745–1815)** | | 1745 Empress Maria Theresa orders the expulsion of Jews from Bohemia and Prague. |
| | 1750 | 1750 Stringent anti-Jewish legislation adopted in Germany: limitation on marriage and increased taxation.<br>1753 British Parliament rejects a proposed law granting certain civic rights to Jews.<br>Major trial of Polish Jews accused of ritual murder. (More than twenty such trials took place in Poland alone between 1700 and 1760.) |
| **Barukh of Medzebozh**<br>**(1757–1811)** | | |
| **Naphtali of Ropshitz**<br>**(1760–1827)** | 1760 | 1763 The twenty-five-year-old philosopher Moses Mendelssohn receives the first prize of the Prussian Academy of Sciences for an essay on metaphysics.<br>1764 "Council of the Four Lands" dissolved. Polish Jews are left without any central organization. |
| | 1770 | 1772 The Mitnagdim, gathered in Vilna, excommunicate the "new sect," the Hasidim.<br>1775 Pius VI's edicts condemn the seven thousand Jews of Rome to misery and public disgrace.<br>1779 Lessing publishes his apologia of Judaism: *Nathan der Weise*. |

| IN THE WORLD AT LARGE | IN THE ARTS |
|---|---|
| | 1726 Swift's *Gulliver's Travels*. |
| 1733–1735 War of the Polish Succession. | 1733 J. S. Bach's B-Minor Mass. |
| 1740–1748 War of the Austrian Succession. | 1740 Hume's *Treatise on Human Nature*.<br>1742 Handel's *Messiah*.<br>1748 Montesquieu's *Spirit of the Laws*. |
| 1756–1763 Seven Year's War. Russia, Austria, France and others against Prussia and Great Britain.<br>1759 Public debate in Lemberg between Frankist renegades and prominent rabbis. | 1759 Inauguration of the British Museum.<br>—— Haydn's First Symphony performed.<br>—— Voltaire's *Candide*. |
| 1760 Beginnings (in England) of the Industrial Revolution.<br>1762–1796 Reign of Catherine II (the Great) of Russia. In the name of the Enlightenment she encourages art, education and letters, and instigates political and social reforms—yet she does nothing to abolish serfdom.<br>1764–1795 Reign of Stanislas II (Poniatowski), last king of Poland. The country is dismembered by Russia, Austria and Prussia during the first | 1762 Rousseau's *Le Contrat Social* and *Émile*.<br>—— Gluck's *Orfeo ed Eurdice* performed. |
| (1772), the second (1793) and the third (1795) partitions. Having no country left to govern, he resigns in 1795.<br>1772 First partition of Poland.<br>1775–1783 American war of independence.<br>1778–1779 War of the Bavarian Succession. | 1771 First publication of *Encyclopaedia Britannica*.<br>1772 Diderot publishes last volume of *Encyclopédie*.<br>1774 Goethe's *Werther*.<br>1779 Lessing's *Nathan der Weise*. |

| | |
|---|---|
| 1780 | 1781  First Jewish Free School opened in Berlin, marking the breakthrough of Jewish *Aufklarung:* Enlightenment.<br>1784  Beginning of publication in Berlin of *Hameassef* (The Gatherer), devoted to rationalist Judaism. |
| 1790 | |
| 1800 | |
| 1810 | 1812  Napoleon's invasion of Russia brings about the emancipation of its Jews.<br>1815  Pius VII reinstitutes the Inquisition. The constitution of Poland—finally formulated—denies civic rights to Jews.<br>1819  Beginning of movement "Wissenschaft des Judentum's" in Germany; it will expand to all of Western Europe. |
| 1820 | 1824  Mass persecutions of Jews in Russia. |

| IN THE WORLD AT LARGE | IN THE ARTS |
|---|---|
| | 1781   Kant's *Critique of Pure Reason*.<br>1785   Mozart's *Marriage of Figaro*. |
| 1789–1799   The French Revolution. | |
| 1793   Second partition of Poland.<br>1793–1794 The Reign of Terror. Robespierre massacres opposition; Marie Antoinette is guillotined.<br>1794   Polish national uprising led by Thaddeus Kosciusko crushed by combined Russian and Prussian armies.<br>1795   Third partition of Poland. Russia, Prussia and Austria absorb the last Polish territories.<br>1796   Napoleon Bonaparte embarks on a series of victories.<br>1799   Napoleon and his army reach the Holy Land. | 1790   Goya's *Caprichos*, works of social satire. Goethe's *Faust*.<br>1797   Chateaubriand's *Essays on Old and Modern Revolutions*. |
| | 1800   Schiller's *Marie Stuart*.<br>1807   Byron publishes his first poems; Fichte, his *Sermons to the German Nation*; Hegel, his *Phenomenology of the Mind*.<br>1808   Beethoven's Pastoral Symphony. |
| 1812   Napoleon invades Russia.<br>1813   Battle of Leipzig—Napoleon defeated.<br>1815   Waterloo. Napoleon defeated and exiled.<br>1814–1815   Congress of Vienna ends wars of Napoleonic era.<br>1815   The Holy Alliance is signed by all European rulers except the King of England, the Pope and the Sultan. Alexander I is the most active sponsor of this agreement, which allies Christian principles with politics and which generally represents a reactionary policy against liberal ideas. | |
| 1825–1855   Reign of Nicholas I of Russia is marked by autocracy and repression of all liberal tendencies. | 1820   Keats publishes his major poems, the *Odes*; Shelley, his *Prometheus Unbound*.<br>1827   Heine's *Das Buch der Lieder*. |

# FIRST CENTERS
# OF HASIDISM

- ○   Principal Centers
- ◎   Major Towns
- —   Provinces

Gdynia ◎
Gdańsk (Danzig) ◎

Niemen

Narew

Bialystok ○

Vistula

Warsaw ○
Ger ●
Kozhenitz ●    Kotzk ◎
Pshiskhe ◎
Lublin ◎
Opatov (Apt) ●
Lizensk ◎    Tomash
Ropshitz ●
(Le

GALICIA

**Inset map:**

BALTIC SEA    RUSSIA

PRUSSIA

LITHUANIA
Kovno
Vilna ●
Minsk ●
Pinsk ●
Pripet
VOLHYNIA
Warsaw ○
Lublin ●
Lwow (Lemberg) ●
Kiev
Cracow
GALICIA    PODOLIA
Ukraine
Dniepr
Dniestr
AUSTRIA
TURKEY

— Poland in 1772    ▰ Poland in 1815

Miles
0

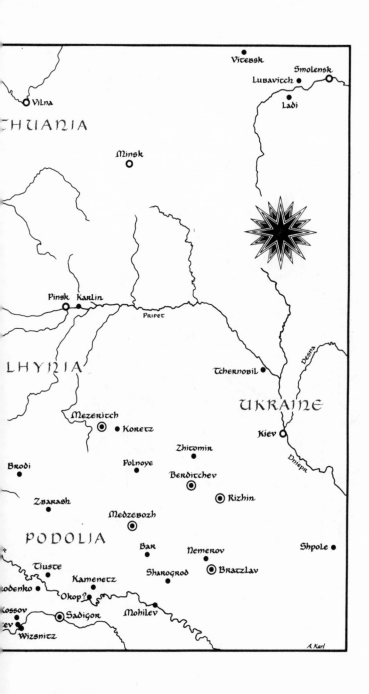

VITEBSK

SMOLENSK
LUBAVITCH
LADI

VILNA

LITHUANIA

MINSK

PINSK KARLIN
PRIPET

VOLHYNIA

TCHERNOBIL

UKRAINE

MEZERITCH
KORETZ
ZHITOMIR
KIEV
BRODI
POLNOYE
BERDITCHEV
ZBARASH
RIZHIN
MEDZEBOZH
PODOLIA
BAR
NEMEROV
SHPOLE
TIUSTE
SHAROGROD
BRATZLAV
KAMENETZ
LODENKO
OKOP?
KOSSOV
MOHILEV
SADIGOR
EV
WIZNITZ

DESNA

DNIEPR

A. Karl

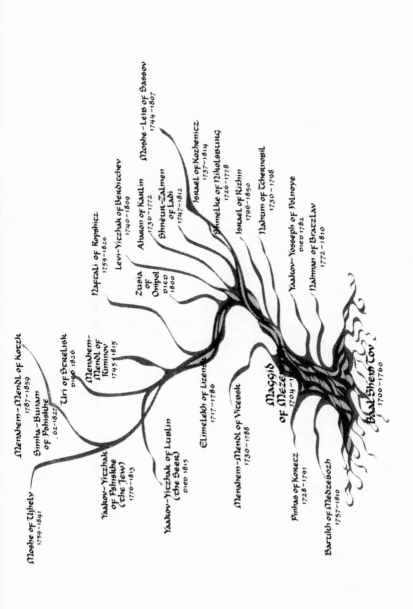

Moshe of Ujhely
1759–1841

Menahem–Mendl of Kotzk
1787–1859

Simha–Bunam
of Pshiskhe
62–1827

Uri of Strelisk
died 1826

Yaakov–Yitzhak
of Pshiskhe
(the Jew)
1770–1813

Menahem–
Mendl of
Riminov
1745–1815

Yaakov–Yitzhak of Lublin
(the Seer)
died 1815

Napftali of Ropshitz
1759–1820

Levi–Yitzhak of Berditchev
1740–1809

Elimelekh of Lizensk
1717–1786

Zusia
of
Ompol
died
1800

Aharon of Karlin
1736–1772

Shneur–Zalmen
of Ladi
1747–1812

Israel of Kozhenicz
1737–1814

Menahem–Mendl of Vitebsk
1730–1788

Shmelke of Nikolasburg
1726–1778

Israel of Rizhin
1796–1850

Maggid
of Mezer...
1704–1...

Nahum of Tchernobil
1730–1798

Yaakov–Yosseph of Polnoye
died 1782

Pinhas of Koretz
1728–1791

Nahman of Bratzlav
1772–1810

Baruch of Medzeboth
1757–1810

Baal Shem Tov
1700–1760

# ABOUT THE AUTHOR

ELIE WIESEL was born in 1928 in the town of Sighet in Transylvania. He was still a child when he was taken from his home and sent to the Auschwitz concentration camp and then to Buchenwald. After the holocaust he lived for eleven years in Paris where he worked as a journalist and a writer. He moved to New York City in 1956 and later became an American citizen. He is married and has one son. His wife, Marion Wiesel, translates his books from the French. He is currently Andrew W. Mellon Professor of Humanities at Boston University.